BGI

7/16

DISCOVERIES IN
SPACE SCIENCE

Stars and
Galaxies

GENERAL EDITORS:
Giles Sparrow, Judith John, and Chris McNab

Cavendish
Square

New York

Published in 2016 by Cavendish Square Publishing, LLC
243 5th Avenue, Suite 136, New York, NY 10016

First Edition

Website: cavendishsq.com

This publication represents the opinions and views of the author based on his or her personal experience, knowledge, and research. The information in this book serves as a general guide only. The author and publisher have used their best efforts in preparing this book and disclaim liability rising directly or indirectly from the use and application of this book.

CPSIA Compliance Information: Batch #CW16CSQ

All websites were available and accurate when this book was sent to press.

Cataloging-in-Publication Data

3 1561 00293 1909

Sparrow, Giles.
Stars and galaxies / edited by Giles Sparrow, Judith John, and Chris McNab.
p. cm. — (Discoveries in space science)
Includes index.
ISBN 978-1-5026-1020-1 (hardcover) ISBN 978-1-5026-1021-8 (ebook)
1. Stars — Juvenile literature. 2. Galaxies — Juvenile literature. I. Sparrow, Giles, 1970-. II. John, Judith. III. McNab, Chris, 1970-. IV. Title.
QB801.7 S63 2016
523.8—d23

Project Editor: Michael Spilling
Design: Hawes Design and Mark Batley
Picture Research: Terry Forshaw
Additional Text: Chris McNab and Judith John

All images are taken from the card set Secrets of the Universe (six volumes) published by International Masters Publishers AB, except the following: NASA and The Hubble Heritage Team (AURA/STScl)/File: V838, Hubble Images.jpg/Wikimedia Commons, cover, 1; NASA, ESA, and the Hubble Heritage Team (STScI/AURA) Acknowledgement: William Blair (Johns Hopkins University)/File:Hubble view of barred spiral galaxy Messier 83.jpg/Wikimedia Commons, 4-5; NASA: 66, 67 both top.

Printed in the United States of America

TABLE OF CONTENTS

DISCOVERIES IN
SPACE SCIENCE

Stars and Galaxies

THE STARS IN THE SKY

Humans have seen patterns in the sky since before recorded history, and many of the star groups and constellations we know today probably date back to these times. At first, constellations were merely the pictures formed by joining certain stars together, but after the invention of the telescope astronomers began to allocate faint stars that fell in no pattern to their nearest constellation. Eventually, in the early twentieth century, the constellations were formalized as eighty-eight distinct regions of the sky with well-defined boundaries. This means that every object in the sky now lies inside a particular constellation. The precise stars we see in our night sky depend on our location on Earth and the time of year—our view of them changes as the Earth orbits the Sun and spins on its own axis, and the Earth itself always blocks our view of half the great "celestial sphere." The Star Atlas pages that follow show the general layout of the constellations and the positions of interesting objects, while many newspapers, magazines, and websites publish monthly maps showing specific locations of the sky in more detail.

STAR ATLASES

Astronomers have been trying for thousands of years to make accurate maps of the night sky. Their efforts have resulted in countless different ways of representing the heavens and nearly as many systems for labeling individual stars, so it is hardly surprising that many star atlases appear confusing to the untrained eye. In fact, the principles of a modern star atlas are really quite simple. Once you get used to the dots, lines, and strange symbols, you'll find that they are indispensable guides to turning our cluttered skies into clear and fascinating areas of study.

POPULAR STAR ATLASES

ATLAS NAME	FAINTEST STAR MAGNITUDE	SCALE (DEGREES PER IN)	NUMBER OF STARS	NUMBER OF MAPS
NORTON'S 2000.0	6.5	7.250	8,400	16
SKY ATLAS 2000.0	8.5	3.120	80,000	26
URANOMETRIA	9.5	1.400	332,000	518
MILLENNIUM STAR ATLAS	11.0	0.705	1,058,000	1,548

MAPPING THE HEAVENS

Star maps and atlases can range from small diagrams in newspapers to large volumes that show hundreds of thousands of stars. But all share one difficulty: how to represent the night sky on a flat sheet of paper when we see it as the inside of a sphere. For a small area this is not too hard, but over a large section of the sky, distortion inevitably creeps in.

Other problems stem from the fact that only half of the celestial sphere is visible from a particular place at any one time, and that the actual part of the sky on view is constantly changing. There is no perfect solution, and there are various ways to divide up the sky. Most are shown here.

Star atlases show the whole sky, section by section, with a reference map to show which part of the sky is visible from the observer's location at each time of the year.

Popular star maps often have lines joining many of the stars. These lines have a double purpose: they show the main star patterns, like the Big Dipper, and they link stars in a particular constellation. Unfortunately, there is no official agreement on where the lines should be placed, and maps can quickly become confusing if they include too many of them.

ONE STAR, SEVERAL NAMES

Stars usually have several different names, most of them provided by the great star catalogs of Johann Bayer (1572–1625) and John Flamsteed (1646–1719). The German Bayer labeled the prominent stars of each constellation with Greek letters in order of brightness: Alpha Centauri, for example, is the brightest star in Centaurus. English astronomer Flamsteed numbered the stars in each constellation from west to east, so 61 Cygni is the sixty-first star in the Cygnus constellation. A third cataloger, the Frenchman Charles Messier (1730–1817), confined his work to star clusters, nebulae, and other deep-space objects now known to be distant galaxies. M 31, for example, is Messier's label for the great galaxy in Andromeda. Most star atlases use the names and numbers provided by all three systems, together with more modern labels for very faint stars.

HEMISPHERIC MAPS

THE SECTION OF SKY VISIBLE FROM EACH PART OF THE EARTH VARIES SLIGHTLY FROM MONTH TO MONTH. HEMISPHERIC MAPS TAKE THIS INTO ACCOUNT AND PROVIDE MONTHLY STAR POSITIONS FOR SPECIFIC LOCATIONS. THEY ARE OFTEN PUBLISHED IN NEWSPAPERS AT THE BEGINNING OF EACH MONTH.

LOOKING BACK

SOME EARLY STAR MAPS TOOK THE FORM OF GLOBES AND WERE ILLUSTRATED WITH THE MYTHICAL FIGURES THAT THE CONSTELLATIONS ARE NAMED FOR. BUT MOST OF THEM SHOWED THE HEAVENS FROM THE OUTSIDE LOOKING IN, SO THE STAR PATTERNS WERE MIRROR IMAGES OF WHAT IS ACTUALLY SEEN IN THE SKY.

BIG ORANGE
The celestial sphere is "peeled" like an orange to create six different map sections.

CIRCULAR SKY
From Earth, the sky appears in the form of a giant sphere.

STAR CATALOG
M-numbers denote Messier-cataloged objects. M 36, M 37, and M 38 are all open star clusters in the Auriga constellation.

SKY GRID
The grid used to mark star positions is equivalent to the Earth's longitude and latitude.

ZOOM IN
Star atlases often include magnifications of interesting areas, such as the Scorpius constellation, shown here.

NO GAPS
Each map section overlaps with its neighbors, so that objects do not fall between them.

SQUASHED STARS
Star positions are distorted as the sphere becomes a sheet.

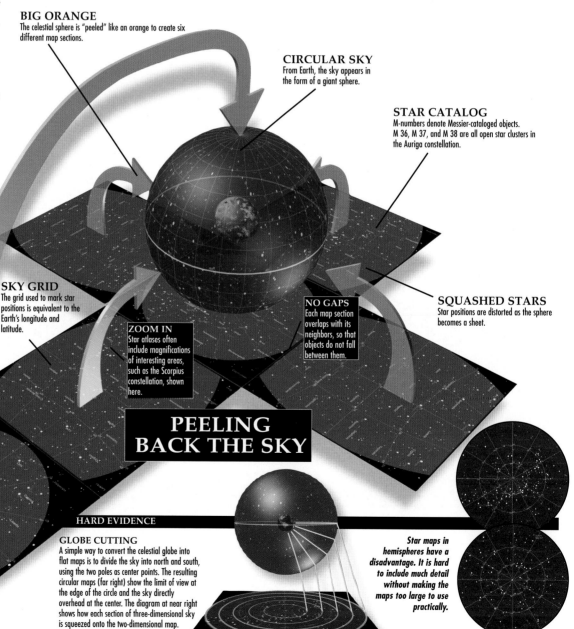

PEELING BACK THE SKY

GLOBE CUTTING
A simple way to convert the celestial globe into flat maps is to divide the sky into north and south, using the two poles as center points. The resulting circular maps (far right) show the limit of view at the edge of the circle and the sky directly overhead at the center. The diagram at near right shows how each section of three-dimensional sky is squeezed onto the two-dimensional map.

Star maps in hemispheres have a disadvantage. It is hard to include much detail without making the maps too large to use practically.

STAR POSITIONS

To find the position of a star or any other celestial object, you need only two coordinates—declination and right ascension, roughly the same as the latitude and longitude of a place on Earth. But the sky appears to rotate daily, which adds a complication, and there are movements of stars to take into account. All this means that star maps, unlike their terrestrial cousins, grow out of date every 50 years or so. In the distant future, our descendants will gaze up at skies quite different from those familiar to us today.

BRIGHTEST STARS

Name	Right Ascension	Declination
Sirius	06 hr 45 min	−16°43'
Canopus	06 hr 24 min	−52°42'
Alpha Centauri	14 hr 40 min	−60°50'
Arcturus	14 hr 16 min	+19°11'
Vega	18 hr 37 min	+38°47'
Capella	05 hr 17 min	+46°00'
Rigel	05 hr 15 min	−08°12'
Procyon	07 hr 39 min	+05°13'
Achernar	01 hr 38 min	−57°14'
Betelgeuse	05 hr 55 min	+07°24'

All positions are given for the epoch 2000.0

HEAVENS ABOVE

The sky appears to us as the inside of a globe, which astronomers call the celestial sphere. As the Earth spins on its axis, the celestial sphere seems to rotate in the opposite direction. But the axis remains fixed throughout the year; any star in particular traces out the same circle around the Earth every day and passes over the same points on Earth.

The sky has its equivalent of the latitude and longitude we use to mark positions on Earth. Celestial latitude is called declination. Stars with a declination of 0° travel along the celestial equator—directly above the Earth's equator; those with declinations of +90° or –90° are always above the Earth's North and South Poles respectively.

To measure longitude in the sky, you need a fixed starting point. This can be anywhere you like, so long as everyone else agrees. On Earth, "longitude zero" is set arbitrarily on Greenwich in London, England; on the celestial sphere, astronomers have chosen the point where the Sun crosses the celestial equator in March.

Known as the first point of Aries, this point marks zero in the sky's longitude system, which astronomers call right ascension. The scale is measured in hours and minutes. The star Regulus, for example, has a right ascension of 10 hours and 8 minutes. So 10 hours and 8 minutes after "zero" has passed above an observer, the sky's rotation will bring the star into view.

CHASING STARS

Like latitude on Earth, declination is measured as an angle: 15° of declination covers 15° of sky. Right ascension is trickier. Because of the direction the sky appears to move in, the scale runs from right to left (from west to east); 24 hours of right ascension cover 360° of the sky. Just as the Earth's lines of longitude vary in their distance apart depending on their latitude, so the size of the sky-circle described by right ascension varies with the declination. On the celestial equator, where the imaginary lines of right ascension are farthest apart, one hour covers a vast area of sky. But near the celestial poles, where the lines

of the sky's "longitude" converge, one hour is able to take in far less space. In each case, though, an hour of right ascension matches 15° of a circle, as well as an hour of real time.

There is another complication. Because the Earth is moving in its orbit, the planet's rotation relative to the stars is slightly faster than its rotation relative to the Sun. In fact, the stars take 23 hours 56 minutes to rotate in the sky, rather than the 24 hours of our solar day. If you time a star crossing your meridian—that is, a north-south line drawn through your position—on one

night, the star will cross it 4 minutes earlier the night after.

Because of this 4-minute difference, astronomers have to employ a separate timescale, called sidereal time, to keep track of star movements. Just as there is a local time for every point on Earth measured by the apparent movement of the Sun, so there is a sidereal time based on the apparent movement of the stars.

Despite these measurements, star maps are only accurate for about 50 years as star positions are subject to an unpredictable and gradual shifting. Stars move through space with their own speeds and in their own directions. Slow variations in the Earth's orbit also affect accuracy.

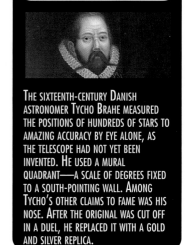

THE CELESTIAL SPHERE

DECLINATION
The sky's "latitude" is measured upward and downward from the celestial equator. The celestial north pole is at +90°, the south pole at –90°.

apparent rotation of the stars

RIGHT ASCENSION
The scale of declination counts eastward in hours and minutes. Its starting point is defined as the place where the Sun passes over the celestial equator in March—known as the first point of Aries.

REGULUS
LEO CONSTELLATION
RIGHT ASCENSION: 10 HR 08 MIN
DECLINATION: +12°

ecliptic: Sun's path

declination

right ascension

ALGENIB
PEGASUS CONSTELLATION
RIGHT ASCENSION: 0 HR 13 MIN
DECLINATION: +15°

first point of Aries

celestial equator

+90° +60° +30° 0° –30° –60° –90°
18 hours 0 hours 12 hours 6 hours

HOT TIP

UNTIL RECENTLY, OBSERVATORIES USED A SEPARATE CLOCK SET TO RUN 4 MINUTES PER DAY SLOWER THAN NORMAL. THE CLOCK KEPT TRACK OF SIDEREAL TIME, WHICH ASTRONOMERS NEED TO KNOW IN ORDER TO POINT THEIR TELESCOPES ACCURATELY. TODAY, ELECTRONIC EQUIPMENT HAS MADE THE SIDEREAL CLOCK OBSOLETE.

HARD EVIDENCE

STAR CRUISER
The fastest-moving star across the sky is the faint Barnard's Star (right), visible in small telescopes. It moves 10.3 arc seconds per year—a Moon diameter every 150 years. Like many local stars, Barnard's is a red dwarf, smaller and dimmer than our Sun. Its speedy apparent motion is due to its proximity. Only six light-years away, Barnard's Star is the third-closest star to Earth, after the Sun and Alpha Centauri.

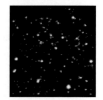

PRECISE DANE

THE SIXTEENTH-CENTURY DANISH ASTRONOMER TYCHO BRAHE MEASURED THE POSITIONS OF HUNDREDS OF STARS TO AMAZING ACCURACY BY EYE ALONE, AS THE TELESCOPE HAD NOT YET BEEN INVENTED. HE USED A MURAL QUADRANT—A SCALE OF DEGREES FIXED TO A SOUTH-POINTING WALL. AMONG TYCHO'S OTHER CLAIMS TO FAME WAS HIS NOSE. AFTER THE ORIGINAL WAS CUT OFF IN A DUEL, HE REPLACED IT WITH A GOLD AND SILVER REPLICA.

MAGNITUDE SCALE

From blazing Sirius to the dimmest members of the Little Dipper, the night sky is littered with stars of different brightnesses. Ancient observers plotted these celestial beacons, taking notice of each light's position, intensity, and color. With the advent of the telescope, many other less-brilliant objects were revealed. More recently, digital cameras and giant optics have plumbed the depths of space, bringing into view stars and galaxies millions of times fainter than those familiar to us in the night

KEY DATES FOR MAGNITUDE

Hipparchus produces his star catalog	129 BCE
Ptolemy's *Almagest* is published	137 CE
Galileo Galilei discovers new stars	1610
Norman Pogson's logarithmic scale	1856
Palomar 200-in (5-m) telescope sees to magnitude 20	1947
Magnitude −22 fireballs observed	1993
Hubble images 30th-magnitude galaxies	1995

LIGHT GAUGE

Around 130 BCE, the Greek astronomer Hipparchus (c. 180–125 BCE) categorized the brightest stars as "first magnitude." This was the first step in creating a system to rank stars in order of brightness. Lesser stars, which were still quite bright, were called second and third magnitude. Combined, these stars made up many of the familiar asterisms of the sky. Fainter stars, scattered throughout the heavens, were similarly rated: fourth and fifth magnitude points in decreasing brightness. Finally, sixth magnitude stars lay at the outer limit of visibility.

After its inclusion in the Egyptian astronomer Ptolemy's (c. 90–168 CE) star atlas, the *Almagest*, the system was adopted unchanged through the Middle Ages—until Galileo turned his telescope toward the heavens and discovered stars fainter than the ones seen with the naked eye. The brightest of these he termed "seventh magnitude."

The current scale encompasses objects with brightness differences of almost 60 magnitudes. The brightest, our Sun, is a blinding magnitude –26.7; the dimmest galaxies glimpsed in long-exposure images captured by the Hubble Space Telescope are estimated to approach magnitude +30. This span represents a huge disparity in brightness—the distant galaxies are some 100 billion trillion times fainter than the Sun.

Fully dark-adapted eyes can see as far down as magnitude 6.5, which encompasses all the planets out to Saturn. A pair of 50-millimeter binoculars reveals ninth magnitude objects, bringing Uranus and Neptune into view; and a 6-inch (152 mm) reflector telescope detects magnitude 13, so Pluto is just visible (if you know just where to look). An amateur with a modest telescope fitted with a CCD (charge coupled device) can see objects down to magnitude 20, a domain long reserved for observatories.

All these magnitudes represent an object's brightness as seen from Earth—its apparent magnitude. This gives no clue to an object's intrinsic brightness. A dim star nearby could have the same apparent magnitude as a bright star that is far away. To compare the real brightness of objects, astronomers use absolute magnitude—a measure of brightness as seen from a standard distance of 32.6 light-years. At that range, our Sun would glow feebly at magnitude 4.85. But the giant star Rigel in the constellation of Orion would shine at –8, rivaling the brightness of the quarter Moon.

Today, devices called photometers can measure to hundredths of a magnitude and can detect subtle changes in a star's output and tiny changes in a planet's albedo (how much sunlight is reflected off the surface), or compare the brightnesses of comets. These precise measurements can give vital clues to the inner structure and workings of the object.

HARD EVIDENCE

WORK IT OUT
You can use a calculator to estimate the brightness difference between our Sun and a given star. First, look up the star's magnitude in a sky atlas and subtract the star's magnitude from –27 (the Sun's magnitude). Then tap in 2.512 and raise it to the power of the difference. For example, a third-magnitude star is 30 magnitudes dimmer than the Sun. Raise 2.512 to the power of 30 and you get a 1 with 12 zeros after it, or a trillion. The star appears a trillion times dimmer than the Sun in the sky.

WHAT IF?

A giant space telescope operated from a permanent space station could glimpse objects at vast distances— and thus events that took place billions of years ago.

...WE COULD SEE FARTHER?

Ever since the advent of the telescope, astronomers have been intent on seeing farther and fainter objects in the depths of space. For two centuries, observers used larger and larger mirrors to probe the cosmos. By the end of the nineteenth century, photography had boosted the telescope's light grasp. The twentieth century saw an instrumentation explosion with the introduction of giant telescopes, smart drives, adaptive optics, CCDs (charge coupled devices), and computer-enhanced imaging. And by the end of the same century, the orbiting Hubble Space Telescope, flying above the atmospheric distortion, had reached down to magnitude +30 by scanning a barren patch of sky for 35 hours straight.

Every time the magnitude barrier is broken and scientists exceed the earlier limit of detection, discoveries are made and insights are gained about the processes that drive the universe. And so the quest for ever fainter objects goes on.

The future promises exciting developments. Further miniaturization of silicon chips—the same process that drives the performance gains of computers—will push the technological limits of digital imaging. Upgraded CCDs attached to the larger replacement for the Hubble Space Telescope will provide further increases in sensitivity, capturing objects a few magnitudes dimmer than currently possible.

Perhaps before the end of the twenty-first century we will see telescopes reaching down to magnitudes as dim as +50. One future development might be that of the ultimate space observatory. With a limiting magnitude of +50, it is hard to imagine what could be dredged up by this enormous eye on the sky. Beneath its gaze would lie planets in other star systems and distant protogalaxies. Perhaps we could see to the edge of the universe—and to the beginning of creation.

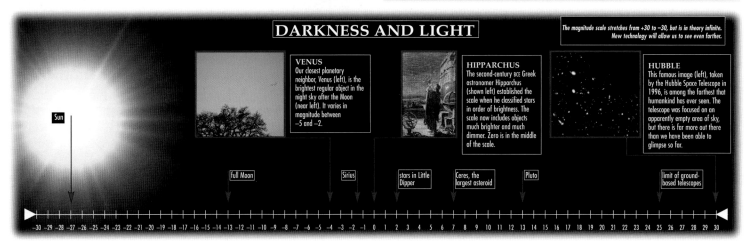

DARKNESS AND LIGHT

The magnitude scale stretches from +30 to –30, but is in theory infinite. New technology will allow us to see even farther.

Sun

VENUS
Our closest planetary neighbor, Venus (left), is the brightest regular object in the night sky after the Moon (near left). It varies in magnitude between –5 and –2.

HIPPARCHUS
The second-century BCE Greek astronomer Hipparchus (shown left) established the scale when he classified stars in order of brightness. The scale now includes objects much brighter and much dimmer. Zero is in the middle of the scale.

HUBBLE
This famous image (left), taken by the Hubble Space Telescope in 1996, is among the farthest that humankind has ever seen. The telescope was focused on an apparently empty area of sky, but there is far more out there than we have been able to glimpse so far.

| full Moon | | Sirius | stars in Little Dipper | Ceres, the largest asteroid | Pluto | | limit of ground-based telescopes |

–30 –29 –28 –27 –26 –25 –24 –23 –22 –21 –20 –19 –18 –17 –16 –15 –14 –13 –12 –11 –10 –9 –8 –7 –6 –5 –4 –3 –2 –1 0 1 2 3 4 5 6 7 8 9 10 11 12 13 14 15 16 17 18 19 20 21 22 23 24 25 26 27 28 29 30

STAR ATLAS 1

To use a star atlas, it helps to imagine that the stars are fixed to the inside of a transparent sphere around the Earth. A star atlas divides this sphere into six sections: one each for the regions around the north and south celestial poles, and four that divide the equatorial regions like the segments of an orange. This section covers the sky from the north celestial pole to a declination of 40° N, describing features that are visible all year from latitudes above 40° N (north of Philadelphia, Pennsylvania, or Madrid, Spain).

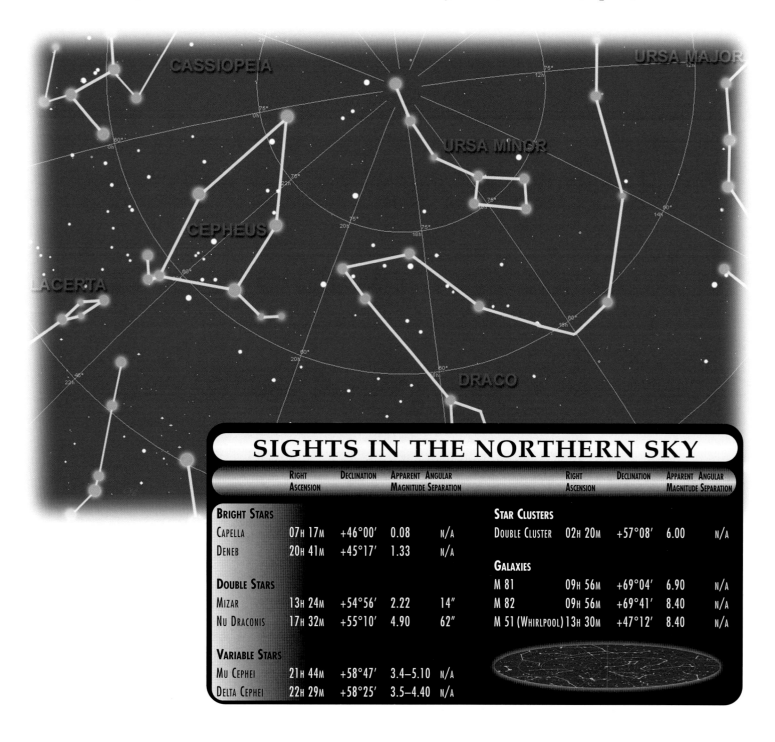

SIGHTS IN THE NORTHERN SKY

	Right Ascension	Declination	Apparent Magnitude	Angular Separation		Right Ascension	Declination	Apparent Magnitude	Angular Separation
Bright Stars					**Star Clusters**				
Capella	07H 17M	+46°00'	0.08	N/A	Double Cluster	02H 20M	+57°08'	6.00	N/A
Deneb	20H 41M	+45°17'	1.33	N/A					
					Galaxies				
Double Stars					M 81	09H 56M	+69°04'	6.90	N/A
Mizar	13H 24M	+54°56'	2.22	14"	M 82	09H 56M	+69°41'	8.40	N/A
Nu Draconis	17H 32M	+55°10'	4.90	62"	M 51 (Whirlpool)	13H 30M	+47°12'	8.40	N/A
Variable Stars									
Mu Cephei	21H 44M	+58°47'	3.4–5.10	N/A					
Delta Cephei	22H 29M	+58°25'	3.5–4.40	N/A					

NORTHERN LIGHTS

Featuring prominently in the northern sky is the group of seven stars that make up the Big Dipper—actually a part of the constellation Ursa Major. Two stars in the bowl of the Dipper, Merak and Dubhe, point to the north pole star, Polaris. On the opposite side of Polaris from the Big Dipper lies the distinctive W-shape of the constellation Cassiopeia.

Because Polaris lies very close to the sky's north pole, the rest of the sky appears to turn counterclockwise around it. The orientation of this map therefore depends on when you look at it. A good tip is to find north, then look around you, halfway up the sky, until you come to Polaris. Follow by searching for either the Big Dipper or Cassiopeia, and turn the map to match the positions of these constellations.

The brightest star in the northern part of the sky is Capella in the constellation of Auriga, with Deneb, in Cygnus, in second place. The Milky Way, which runs through Cassiopeia, is almost overhead on winter evenings.

KEMBLE'S CASCADE

With binoculars, look for a shaft of starlight in the constellation of Camelopardalis (the Giraffe). Kemble's Cascade consists of a chain of about 20 stars, the brightest of which is fifth magnitude, and spans five Moon widths. Canadian astronomer Lucian Kemble described it in 1980 as "a beautiful cascade of faint stars, tumbling from the northeast down to the open cluster NGC 1502." To find it, begin at the bright stars of Perseus and hop north from star to star until you see the fifth magnitude star at the Cascade's center.

M 81 AND M 82

A pair of contrasting galaxies are within range of small telescopes in the northern part of Ursa Major, about a third of the way from the bowl of the Big Dipper to the Pole Star. M 81 is a beautiful, symmetrically shaped spiral galaxy. It covers nearly half the area of the full Moon, but is tilted at an angle to us so that its outline appears almost elliptical. Half a degree to the north of it is situated M

82, smaller and fainter but still detectable in binoculars on a good night. M 82 is also elliptical, and is at right angles to M 81. M 82 is thought to be interacting with a large cloud of dust, which can give it a strange appearance on long-exposure photographs.

POLARIS

Contrary to popular myth, the north pole star, Polaris, is not especially bright. In fact, it is an ordinary-looking star of second magnitude that is special only because it happens to lie within a degree of the north celestial pole. Small telescopes show that Polaris is the brightest member of a roughly circular chain of stars, like a necklace, about one full Moon width wide. Polaris is actually classified as a Cepheid variable, but its brightness changes are so slight that they are not noticeable with the naked eye.

The map covers areas of the sky around the celestial north pole (below, shaded).

Magnitude Scale
0
1
2
3
4
5

Numbers around the edge of the map are hours of right ascension. Numbers in the middle are degrees of declination.

STAR ATLAS 2

This section covers the region of sky between declination 50° N and 50° S, and from right ascension 21 hours to 3 hours. Running vertically through the center of this area is the line marking zero-hours right ascension, the sky's equivalent of the Greenwich meridian. The zero line runs from the celestial poles through the point where the Sun crosses the celestial equator from south to north each year. The stars in this part of the sky are visible in the evening from September through to December.

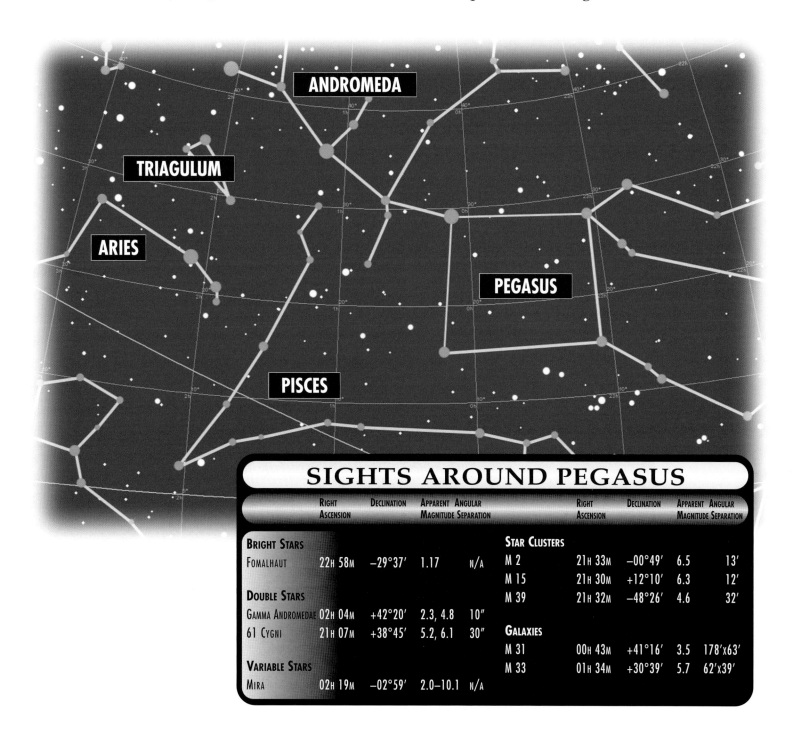

SIGHTS AROUND PEGASUS

	Right Ascension	Declination	Apparent Magnitude	Angular Separation		Right Ascension	Declination	Apparent Magnitude	Angular Separation
Bright Stars					**Star Clusters**				
Fomalhaut	22H 58M	−29°37′	1.17	N/A	M 2	21H 33M	−00°49′	6.5	13′
					M 15	21H 30M	+12°10′	6.3	12′
Double Stars					M 39	21H 32M	−48°26′	4.6	32′
Gamma Andromedae	02H 04M	+42°20′	2.3, 4.8	10″					
61 Cygni	21H 07M	+38°45′	5.2, 6.1	30″	**Galaxies**				
					M 31	00H 43M	+41°16′	3.5	178′x63′
Variable Stars					M 33	01H 34M	+30°39′	5.7	62′x39′
Mira	02H 19M	−02°59′	2.0–10.1	N/A					

NORTHERN FALL SKIES

This area of sky is strangely bereft of bright objects. The only first magnitude star is Fomalhaut, in the constellation Piscis Austrinus. Dominating this area is the Square of Pegasus, which stands astride the zero-hour line of right ascension. The Square is a block of sky with a moderately bright star at each corner. From mid-northern latitudes, the Square stands high in the south on November evenings. A line southward from the western edge of the Square leads to Fomalhaut. Northwest of the Square is Cygnus, a summer constellation now departing the evening sky.

Draw a line northward from the eastern side of the Square and you will come to the W-shape of stars that marks the position of the constellation Cassiopeia and, in the north-eastern corner, her daughter Andromeda.

NGC 253

The constellation of Sculptor contains the south pole of our galaxy, the point that lies at 90° south of the plane of the Milky Way. In this direction, we can see out into deep space without interruption from stars, gas, or dust clouds in our own galaxy. The most prominent galaxies in Sculptor are NGC 55, on its southern border, and NGC 253 (inset), almost on its northern border with Cetus. Both are spiral galaxies tilted to us at such an angle that they appear elongated. NGC 253, the brighter of the two, can be picked up in binoculars under favorable conditions. Moderate size telescopes show that NGC 253 has a mottled appearance, which was caused by dust clouds in its arms.

NGC 891

A galaxy of interest in the constellation of Andromeda is NGC 891 (top inset), a spiral seen almost exactly edge-on. Lying near the border with Perseus, it can be glimpsed in moderate-size telescopes as a hazy tenth-magnitude band of light one-third the apparent diameter of the Moon.

Larger telescopes—with apertures of 12 inches (300 mm) or more—may show a dark lane of dust that runs across the galaxy, but this feature is best seen on long-exposure photographs.

M 39

The large open star cluster M 39 can be found high in the sky in the eastern edge of Cygnus (at the top right of the main map). It is bright enough to be glimpsed with the naked eye under clear conditions. Binoculars show its most prominent members (inset), of seventh magnitude, while through small telescopes about two dozen stars can be seen, with the same apparent width as the full Moon. M 39 lies 950 light-years away.

ARABIAN NIGHTS

Many civilizations in history have had their own star myths and constellation figures, with the present system only accepted in 1930. Although most constellations are Greek in origin, many stars have Arabic names, showing that Arabic astronomy was once dominant.

As most of Europe entered the so-called Dark Ages—when much of the knowledge built up by the Greeks and Romans was lost—the nations of Islam became the center of astronomical knowledge.

Perhaps the most influential Arabic astronomer was Abd al-Rahman al-Sufi (903–986 CE),

known as Azophi. Around 964 CE, he produced an Arabic edition of the Greek star atlas the *Almagest*, in which he introduced many star names. Some came from tribes, but others were Arabic versions of Ptolemy's descriptions. As Arabic influence spread into Spain from the tenth century ---, the works of Ptolemy (90–168), the author of the *Almagest*, were reintroduced to European scholars. Greek and Arab books were translated from Arabic into Latin, the scientific language of the day.

By this roundabout route, we now have constellations of Greek origin bearing Latin titles and containing stars with Arabic names.

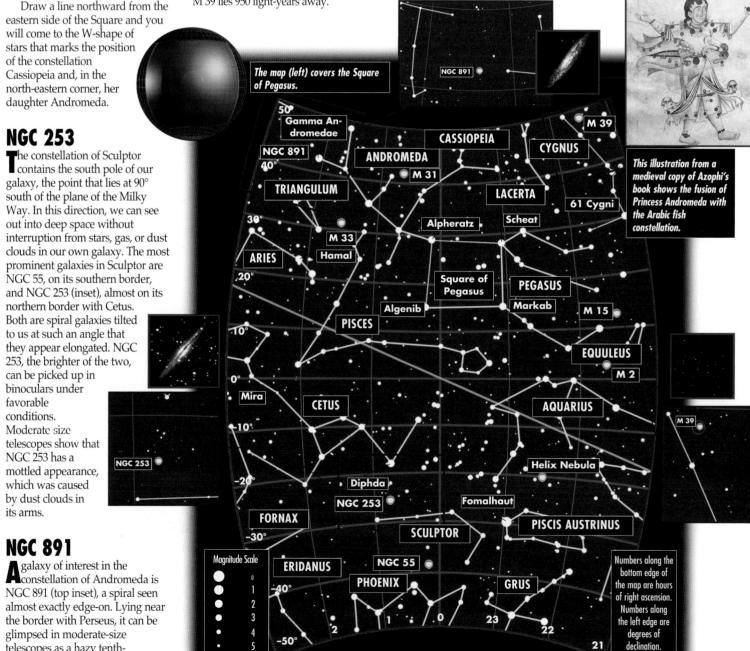

The map (left) covers the Square of Pegasus.

This illustration from a medieval copy of Azophi's book shows the fusion of Princess Andromeda with the Arabic fish constellation.

Numbers along the bottom edge of the map are hours of right ascension. Numbers along the left edge are degrees of declination.

16

STAR ATLAS 3

This section covers the region of the sky from three hours to nine hours right ascension, and between declination 50° north and 50° south. Running down the center of this area from north to south is the six-hour line of right ascension, which passes just to the east of the bright star Betelgeuse. The Sun crosses this six-hour line at the June solstice each year. This part of the sky is visible in the evening from December to March—making it winter in the northern hemisphere and summer in the southern hemisphere.

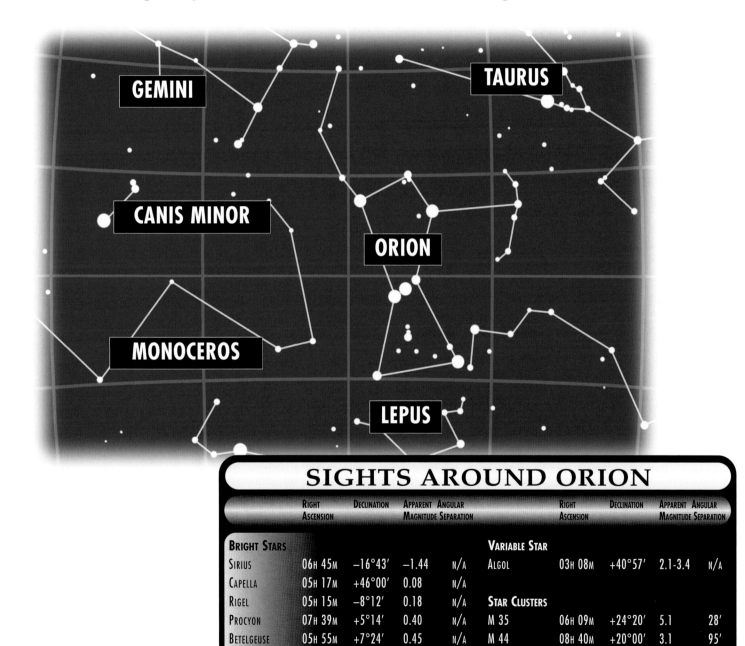

SIGHTS AROUND ORION

	Right Ascension	Declination	Apparent Magnitude	Angular Separation		Right Ascension	Declination	Apparent Magnitude	Angular Separation
Bright Stars					**Variable Star**				
Sirius	06H 45M	−16°43′	−1.44	N/A	Algol	03H 08M	+40°57′	2.1-3.4	N/A
Capella	05H 17M	+46°00′	0.08	N/A					
Rigel	05H 15M	−8°12′	0.18	N/A	**Star Clusters**				
Procyon	07H 39M	+5°14′	0.40	N/A	M 35	06H 09M	+24°20′	5.1	28′
Betelgeuse	05H 55M	+7°24′	0.45	N/A	M 44	08H 40M	+20°00′	3.1	95′
Double Star					**Nebula**				
Castor	07H 36M	+31°51′	1.9, 3.0	3″	M 1	05H 35M	+22°01′	8.4	16′x4′

ORION'S CONSORT

Straddling the celestial equator, the constellation Orion takes center stage, surrounded by Taurus, Auriga, Gemini, and Canis Major. This is one of the most glorious areas of the sky, containing five of the 10 brightest stars in the heavens: Sirius, Capella, Rigel, Procyon, and Betelgeuse. South of the three stars of Orion's belt is a complex of stars and gas clouds that form his sword, most notably the Orion Nebula. Follow the line of Orion's belt to the northwest and you will come to the V-shaped Hyades star cluster in Taurus. To its southeast the belt points to Sirius in Canis Major, the brightest star in the entire night sky. Northeast of Orion is Gemini, with its brightest stars Castor and Pollux, while north of Orion lies Auriga and its leading star Capella. To the southwest of Orion the long constellation of Eridanus, the river, meanders into the southern sky.

THE TRAPEZIUM

At the heart of the Orion Nebula is a multiple star known as Theta Orionis, popularly called the Trapezium because its four brightest stars are arranged in a trapezium shape (an irregular quadrilateral). Actually a small cluster of stars, Theta Orionis (below) was born from the gas of the Orion Nebula within the past few million years, and the light of the newborn stars makes the nebula glow. Small telescopes show the four brightest components of Theta Orionis, of magnitudes 5.1, 6.7, 6.7, and 7.9, but a telescope with a 4-inch (100 mm) aperture or larger also reveals two others. Nearby lies Theta-2 Orionis.

M 78

Attention on nebulosity in Orion often focuses on the glorious Orion Nebula and the faint but fascinating Horsehead Nebula to its north. Consequently, the patch of nebulosity known as M 78 (below) is often overlooked. Unlike most bright nebulae, it is not composed of glowing gas, but is lit up by starlight reflected off dust. In moderate apertures it resembles the head of a comet with a short tail. A tenth-magnitude double star appears at the "comet's" head.

M 79

The beautiful globular cluster M 79 is notable for its unusual position. Most globular clusters are situated close to the center of the galaxy. But M 79 (below) lies in the opposite hemisphere of the sky from the Galactic Center. This is because the cluster is actually beyond us from the perspective of the Galactic Center: it is about 41,000 light-years from us, but about 60,000 light-years from the Galactic Center.

STARS OF HISTORY

To the ancient Greeks, Orion was a great hunter, but other cultures saw the constellation differently. In ancient Egypt, Orion represented Osiris, god of the underworld, who was killed by his brother before becoming immortal.

In China, Orion was seen as the leading warrior appointed by the local farmers to defend their food against raiders during the winter. For Hindus, the three belt stars formed an arrow, shot by the deer slayer, Lubdhaka, whose bow is represented by Sirius and nearby stars. Native Peruvians saw the three stars of Orion as a criminal held by the arms, with the four stars outlining the body of Orion as vultures about to tear him apart.

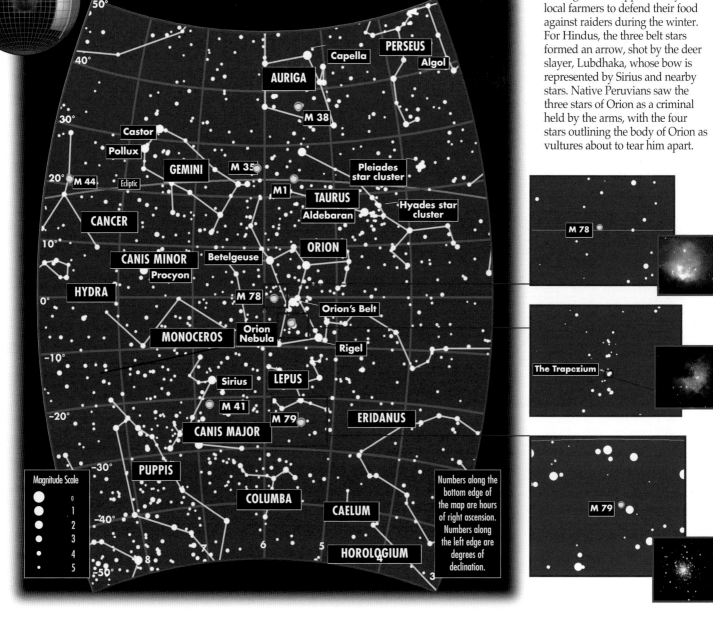

This map covers the area of sky around the constellation of Orion

Numbers along the bottom edge of the map are hours of right ascension. Numbers along the left edge are degrees of declination.

18

STAR ATLAS 4

This section covers the region of the sky from right ascension nine hours to 15 hours, and between declination 50° north and 50° south. Running north to south through the center of this area is the 12-hour line of right ascension, which brushes the tail of Leo before heading into the southern celestial hemisphere. The Sun crosses this 12-hour line at the September equinox each year. This part of the sky is visible from March until June—spring in the northern hemisphere and fall in the southern hemisphere.

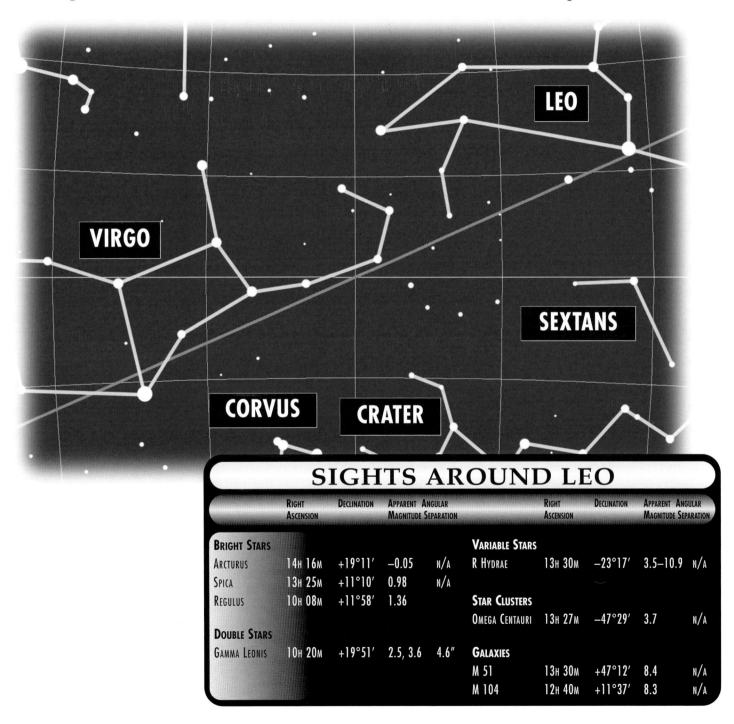

SIGHTS AROUND LEO

	Right Ascension	Declination	Apparent Magnitude	Angular Separation		Right Ascension	Declination	Apparent Magnitude	Angular Separation
Bright Stars					**Variable Stars**				
Arcturus	14H 16M	+19°11′	−0.05	N/A	R Hydrae	13H 30M	−23°17′	3.5–10.9	N/A
Spica	13H 25M	+11°10′	0.98	N/A					
Regulus	10H 08M	+11°58′	1.36		**Star Clusters**				
					Omega Centauri	13H 27M	−47°29′	3.7	N/A
Double Stars									
Gamma Leonis	10H 20M	+19°51′	2.5, 3.6	4.6″	**Galaxies**				
					M 51	13H 30M	+47°12′	8.4	N/A
					M 104	12H 40M	+11°37′	8.3	N/A

LION'S DEN

This area of sky is ruled by Leo, its head marked by a sickle-shape of stars with the brightest, Regulus, at the base. Blue-white Regulus is at the apex of a long, thin triangle of stars completed by Arcturus in Boötes and Spica in Virgo. The orange-colored Arcturus, harbinger of spring, also helps form another pattern: a large starry "Y," made up of Epsilon Boötis (Izar) in the middle, Alpha Coronae Borealis (Alphecca) at top left, and Gamma Boötis (Seginus) at top right.

South of Leo, the constellation of Hydra, the Water Snake, slithers across 100° of sky from its head, adjoining Cancer and Canis Minor, to the tip of its tail, next to Libra. Beneath the tail of Hydra, lies the Centaurus, the Centaur, boasting the largest and brightest globular cluster in the sky, Omega Centauri.

M 68

To find this eighth-magnitude globular cluster, draw a line southward from Delta through Beta Corvi to reach a fifth-magnitude double star. M 68 is about a Moon's width away. Visible as a fuzzy star in binoculars, it shows up in small telescopes at about 10 times the diameter of Jupiter. This extremely rich globular contains over 100,000 stars, and would appear far more impressive were it not over 30,000 light-years away. Some of its outlying stars appear to be in loops, but apertures of at least 4 inches (100 mm) are needed to see this.

M 84 AND M 86

Near the heart of the Virgo cluster lie two of its main members. M 84 is classed as an elliptical galaxy, but it may in fact be a lenticular galaxy, class S0—halfway between an elliptical and a spiral. M 86, an elliptical galaxy, is the larger of the pair, with a more distinct edge than the hazier M 84. Both M 84 and M 86 can be seen through a 3-inch (76 mm) telescope, and is surrounded with faint galaxies.

M 105

Galaxy hunters will be familiar with the pairings of M 65 and M 66, and M 95 and M 96. The latter duo has a third companion which is often overlooked. M 105, a ninth-magnitude elliptical galaxy that appears almost perfectly rounded and featureless except for its star-like core. Small telescopes will show it, while somewhat larger apertures will also detect two fainter galaxies with which it forms a triangle, NGC 3384 and—faintest of the trio—NGC 3389. All these galaxies are thought to be members of a related group.

A DIFFERENT STORY

To modern-day observers, the stars of Leo outline the shape of a lion, but other civilizations saw them differently. For example, about 4,000 years ago, the ancient Babylonians interpreted the stars of Leo as a huge dog, representing the ferocious guard dogs they used for protection. Elsewhere, the sickle of Leo has been seen as a figure, such as in Siberia, where the shape of a sleeping woman was seen in its arc of stars, with the top of the sickle her head and Regulus her knees. In China, the arc of the sickle was extended to the north to complete the Rain Dragon, an effigy of which was carried at times of drought. In another Chinese grouping, the star at the root of Leo's tail, Denebola, represented the Chinese Royal Prince, and the surrounding stars were his extensive retinue of advisors and guards.

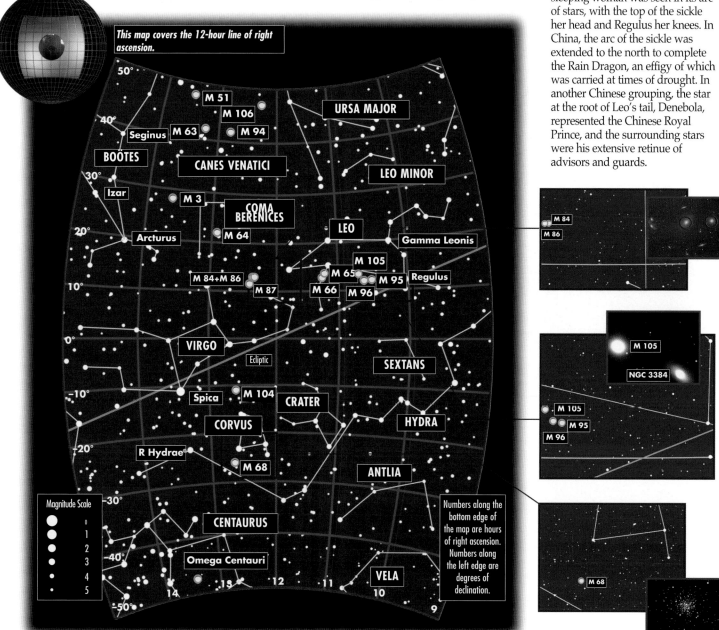

This map covers the 12-hour line of right ascension.

Numbers along the bottom edge of the map are hours of right ascension. Numbers along the left edge are degrees of declination.

Magnitude Scale
0
1
2
3
4
5

STAR ATLAS 5

This atlas covers the sky from right ascension 15 hours to 21 hours, and between declinations 50° north and 50° south. Running vertically straight through the center of this area is the 18-hour line of right ascension, which the Sun crosses at the December solstice each year, when it is at its farthest south of the celestial equator. This part of the sky is visible in the evening from the months of June until September—during summer in the northern hemisphere and winter in the southern hemisphere—and also includes the brightest and richest parts of the Milky Way.

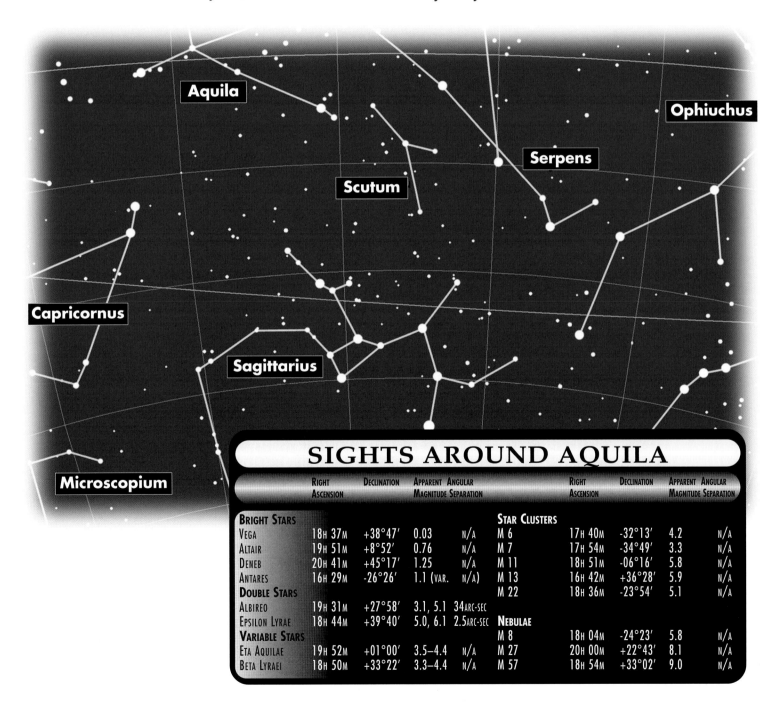

SIGHTS AROUND AQUILA

	Right Ascension	Declination	Apparent Magnitude	Angular Separation		Right Ascension	Declination	Apparent Magnitude	Angular Separation
Bright Stars					**Star Clusters**				
Vega	18H 37M	+38°47'	0.03	N/A	M 6	17H 40M	-32°13'	4.2	N/A
Altair	19H 51M	+8°52'	0.76	N/A	M 7	17H 54M	-34°49'	3.3	N/A
Deneb	20H 41M	+45°17'	1.25	N/A	M 11	18H 51M	-06°16'	5.8	N/A
Antares	16H 29M	-26°26'	1.1 (var.)	N/A)	M 13	16H 42M	+36°28'	5.9	N/A
Double Stars					M 22	18H 36M	-23°54'	5.1	N/A
Albireo	19H 31M	+27°58'	3.1, 5.1	34ARC-SEC					
Epsilon Lyrae	18H 44M	+39°40'	5.0, 6.1	2.5ARC-SEC	**Nebulae**				
Variable Stars					M 8	18H 04M	-24°23'	5.8	N/A
Eta Aquilae	19H 52M	+01°00'	3.5–4.4	N/A	M 27	20H 00M	+22°43'	8.1	N/A
Beta Lyraei	18H 50M	+33°22'	3.3–4.4	N/A	M 57	18H 54M	+33°02'	9.0	N/A

NORTHERN SKIES

Two giants stand head-to-head in the summer sky: Hercules and Ophiuchus. The constellation Hercules represents the Greek demigod famous for undertaking twelve nearly impossible tasks to free himself from servitude. Ophiuchus is less well-known, representing the Greek god of medicine. In the sky he is visualized with a huge snake wrapped around him, in the form of the constellation Serpens. Serpens is divided into two halves, one representing the head (Serpens Caput) and the other its tail (Serpens Cauda), but the snake is a single constellation.

A different sort of giant in this part of the sky is the giant trio of stars known as the Summer Triangle: Vega in Lyra, Deneb in Cygnus, and Altair in Aquila. Vega, the brightest, is a blue-white star that is the first to come into view as the sky darkens. A summer treat is to scan this area with binoculars, picking out the deep-sky objects.

LAGOON NEBULA

The Lagoon Nebula in Sagittarius, also known as M 8, is an elongated cloud of gas visible to the naked eye on clear nights and easily seen in binoculars. One half of the nebula contains the open cluster NGC 6530, composed of about two dozen stars of seventh magnitude and fainter, while in the other half burns the hot sixth-magnitude blue supergiant 9 Sagittarii, one of the main stars that lights up the nebula.

M 56

Lying nearly halfway between Beta Cygni (Albireo) and Gamma Lyrae, this globular cluster in Lyra is one of the fainter deep-sky objects listed by Charles Messier. It is not difficult to find, but at eighth magnitude it is beyond the range of most binoculars. Small to moderate-size telescopes show a hazy patch elongated north-south, without the strong central condensation common in many globulars. Larger apertures and higher powers resolve individual stars, shown as chains and arcs.

NGC 6572

This eighth-magnitude planetary nebula can be seen in a 3-inch (75 mm) telescope, lying in a fairly barren area in the north of Ophiuchus near the border with Serpens Cauda. Its disk is small—about 8 arc seconds wide, twice the apparent size of Uranus, and with a similar blue-green color. It lies at the end of a chain of faint stars.

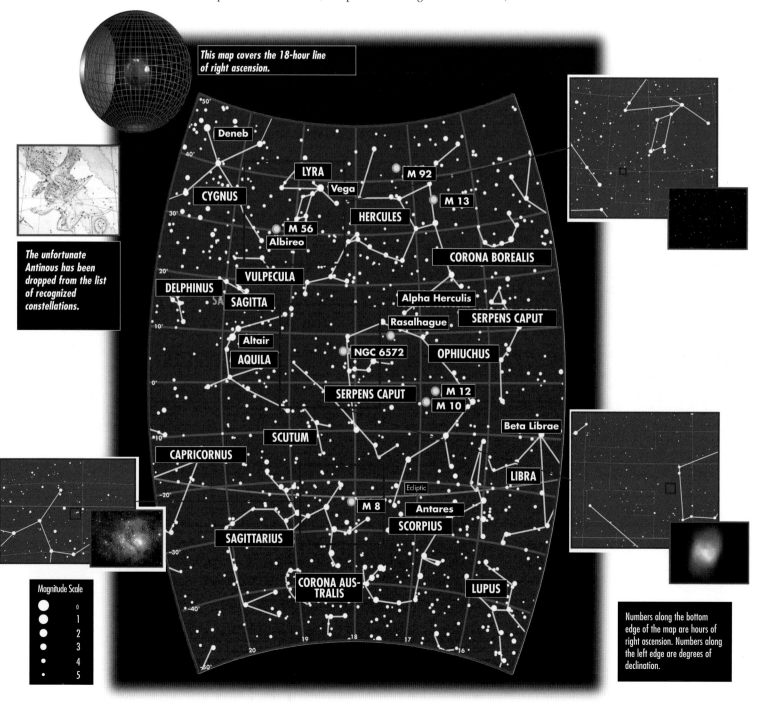

This map covers the 18-hour line of right ascension.

The unfortunate Antinous has been dropped from the list of recognized constellations.

Deneb · LYRA · M 92 · Vega · CYGNUS · HERCULES · M 13 · M 56 · Albireo · CORONA BOREALIS · VULPECULA · DELPHINUS · SAGITTA · Alpha Herculis · Rasalhague · SERPENS CAPUT · Altair · NGC 6572 · OPHIUCHUS · AQUILA · SERPENS CAPUT · M 12 · M 10 · SCUTUM · Beta Librae · CAPRICORNUS · LIBRA · Ecliptic · M 8 · Antares · SAGITTARIUS · SCORPIUS · CORONA AUS-TRALIS · LUPUS

Magnitude Scale
0
1
2
3
4
5

Numbers along the bottom edge of the map are hours of right ascension. Numbers along the left edge are degrees of declination.

22

STAR ATLAS 6

This section covers the sky from declination 40° S to the south celestial pole, an area that is mostly invisible from the United States, although regions at the edge of the map can be seen from the southern states. This area contains the second- and third-brightest stars in the night sky, Canopus and Alpha Centauri, which is also the closest naked-eye star to the Sun. Other great naked-eye sights include the Southern Cross and the Magellanic Clouds, two small irregular galaxies that are satellites of our Milky Way.

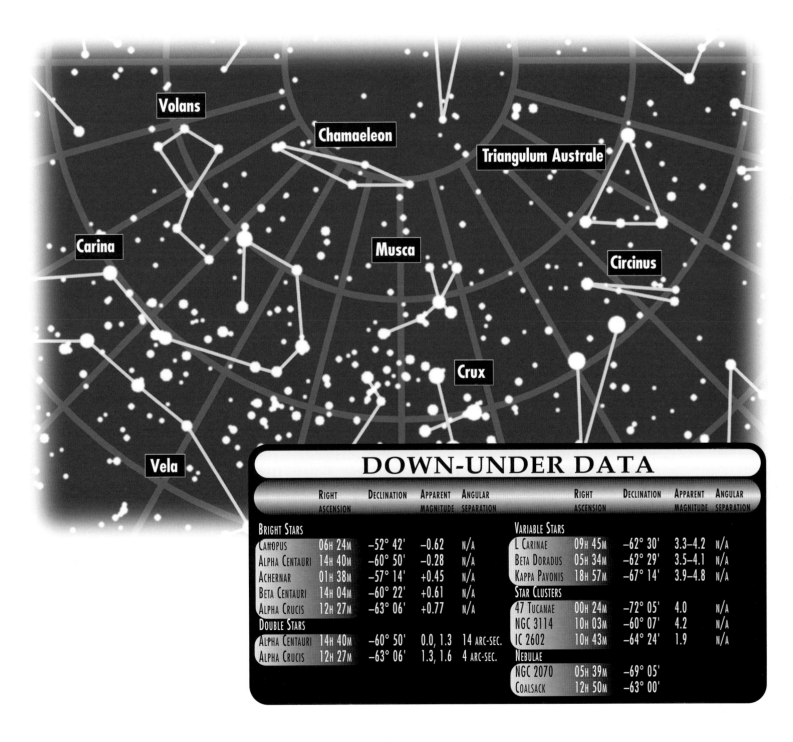

DOWN-UNDER DATA

	Right Ascension	Declination	Apparent Magnitude	Angular Separation		Right Ascension	Declination	Apparent Magnitude	Angular Separation
Bright Stars					**Variable Stars**				
Canopus	06H 24M	−52° 42'	−0.62	N/A	L Carinae	09H 45M	−62° 30'	3.3–4.2	N/A
Alpha Centauri	14H 40M	−60° 50'	−0.28	N/A	Beta Doradus	05H 34M	−62° 29'	3.5–4.1	N/A
Achernar	01H 38M	−57° 14'	+0.45	N/A	Kappa Pavonis	18H 57M	−67° 14'	3.9–4.8	N/A
Beta Centauri	14H 04M	−60° 22'	+0.61	N/A	**Star Clusters**				
Alpha Crucis	12H 27M	−63° 06'	+0.77	N/A	47 Tucanae	00H 24M	−72° 05'	4.0	N/A
Double Stars					NGC 3114	10H 03M	−60° 07'	4.2	N/A
Alpha Centauri	14H 40M	−60° 50'	0.0, 1.3	14 arc-sec.	IC 2602	10H 43M	−64° 24'	1.9	N/A
Alpha Crucis	12H 27M	−63° 06'	1.3, 1.6	4 arc-sec.	**Nebulae**				
					NGC 2070	05H 39M	−69° 05'		
					Coalsack	12H 50M	−63° 00'		

SOUTHERN BEAUTIES

The symbol of the southern skies is Crux, the constellation of the Southern Cross, which is depicted on several national flags. It contains four bright stars arranged in cruciform shape with a fifth, fainter star just off-center. The brightest, Alpha Crucis, is actually a sparkling double star, easily seen by a small telescope. It is also the closest first-magnitude star to the southern pole. Two other bright stars, Alpha and Beta Centauri, point toward Crux. Alpha Centauri, the third-brightest star in the sky, is another easy double for small telescopes.

The long axis of the Southern Cross points toward the south celestial pole. On the opposite side of the pole from Crux lie the large and small Magellanic Clouds (LMC and SMC), two small satellites of our own galaxy. Binoculars show many clusters and nebulae within them. The most prominent is the Tarantula Nebula in the LMC.

NGC 3114

This large and scattered open cluster in Carina, of similar apparent size to the full Moon, is visible to the naked eye in dark skies. Its brightest members, of sixth magnitude and fainter, can easily be seen in binoculars. Small

telescopes, with wide field and low magnification, show its stars to be arranged in curving arms somewhat like a very sparse spiral galaxy.

NGC 6752

At sixth magnitude, this globular cluster in Pavo can be seen in binoculars and is close enough to us—about 15,000 light-years away—for its brightest stars to be resolvable in telescopes of 3 inches (76 mm) in aperture. The condensed central part appears about four times larger than the disk of Jupiter, while its scattered outlying stars extend over half the apparent diameter of the Moon.

COALSACK

The best-known and most prominent of all dark nebulae, the Coalsack is a cloud of dust and gas about 600 light-years away in the local spiral arm of our galaxy. The Coalsack blots out light from the stars behind. Its prominence is due

to it being silhouetted against a particularly rich backdrop of the Milky Way near the stars of Crux. Easily visible with the naked eye, the Coalsack is shaped like an almond and spans the width of a dozen full Moons.

NEW INVENTIONS IN THE SKIES

Most of the area of sky around the south celestial pole was unknown to European astronomers prior to the fifteenth century, when European seamen ventured into the southern hemisphere, crossing the Atlantic to South America, and around the southern tip of Africa. They returned with reports of new celestial sights such as the two satellites now known as the Magellanic Clouds, after the Portuguese round-the-world explorer Ferdinand Magellan.

But the southern stars were not grouped into new constellations until around 1600, when two Dutch navigators, Pieter Dirkszoon Keyser and Frederick de Houtman, introduced twelve figures named mostly after exotic animals.

The first comprehensive southern sky survey was made around 150 years later by a Frenchman, Nicolas Louis de Lacaille. From the Cape of Good Hope in southern Africa between 1751 and 1752, Lacaille cataloged nearly 10,000 stars (Keyser and de Houtman had charted only about 300 of the brightest stars), introducing fourteen new constellations to fill in the gaps between Keyser and de Houtman's figures.

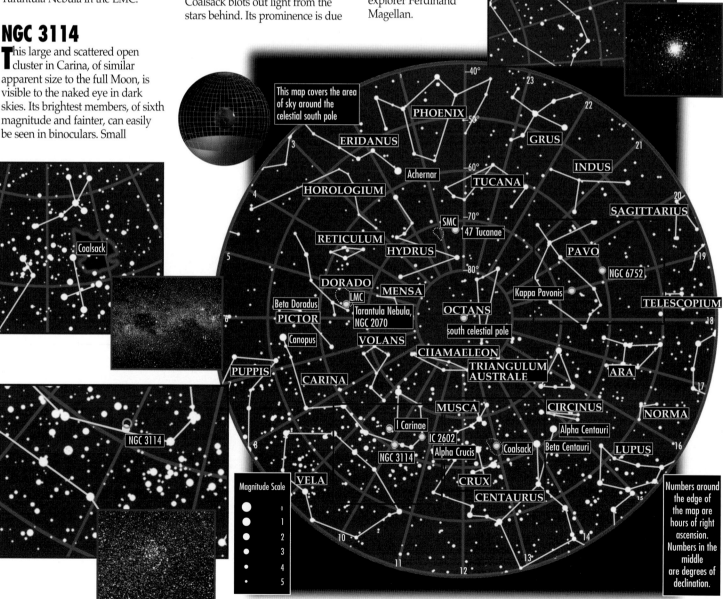

The Hubble Space Telescope floats against the background of Earth after a week of essential repair and upgrade by Space Shuttle *Columbia* astronauts in 2002. Astronauts also installed a new camera—the Advanced Camera for Surveys—which doubled Hubble's field of view.

STUDYING THE STARS

Apart from the Sun, all the stars lie so far away that they only appear as points of light through even the most powerful telescopes. In order to understand the physical properties of stars, and explain how and why they differ from one another, astronomers must use every technique at their disposal to extract information from starlight. They observe not just in visible light, but at a variety of other wavelengths of radiation—in parts of the spectrum where objects cooler or hotter than the Sun may shine. Radio waves and infrared are emitted by some of the coolest objects in the universe, while ultraviolet, X-rays, and gamma rays, with far more energy than the Sun's surface. By splitting the radiation from celestial objects into a spectrum of different wavelengths, astronomers can determine the elements that emit the radiation and can even measure the motions of individual stars. All this information ultimately allows them to model the true physical properties of stars and to find patterns in these properties that are the key to understanding stellar evolution.

MESSAGES IN STARLIGHT

The starlight that twinkles from a clear night sky has reached the end of a journey that may have taken thousands of years—and the light bears the marks of its passage. It has been dimmed, colored, and distorted during its trip through space. In recompense, though, starlight is crammed with information. It can tell scientists much about the star that created it. And for those who can read the code, starlight also tells tales of the molecules, atoms, and magnetic fields it has encountered since its birth.

HISTORY OF STARLIGHT

1836 . .British astronomer John Herschel and German physicist Karl August von Steinheil independently devise instruments to compare the brightnesses of stars.

1864 . .William Huggins and Angelo Secchi independently begin the study of stellar spectra.

1868 . .William Huggins measures speed at which Sirius is moving away from us by the Doppler shift in its spectrum

1868 . .Spectrum of hitherto unknown element discovered in sunlight. The element is named helium (from the Greek *helios*, meaning "sun") and is discovered on Earth in 1895.

1904 . .Existence of interstellar gas discovered from absorption lines in star spectra.

1929 . .Edwin Hubble discovers the expansion of the universe from the redshifts of light from galaxies.

1930 . .Robert Trumpler discovers the extent of interstellar light absorption by observing globular clusters.

1969 . .First organic molecule, formaldehyde, discovered in interstellar gas from its spectral lines.

1970 . .Molecular hydrogen observed in space by its spectrum (radio astronomers had already mapped hydrogen in the form of single atoms).

SPECTRAL STORIES

Starlight is born in the core of a star. At temperatures of millions of degrees and pressures of hundreds of billions of atmospheres, nuclear reactions release photons of intensely energetic gamma rays. As these fight their way outward through the star—a journey that can take millions of years—they are constantly absorbed and reemitted, usually at a lower energy level. Lastly, at the stellar surface, where the temperature is measured only in thousands or tens of thousands of degrees, the photons begin their trip through space. No longer gamma rays, most of them appear as heat and pressure.

The color of that light is the first important message that it bears. The hotter the star's surface, the shorter the wavelength. The star Rigel, for example, looks distinctly blue: it has a temperature of 20,000°F (11,000°C). The red color of Betelgeuse indicates a surface temperature of only 6,000°F (3,300°C), and stars with temperatures close to that of the Sun, about 10,000°F (5,500°C), appear white.

Astronomers gain far more information when they examine the spectrum of the starlight. Split rainbow-style into its component colors, the light reveals its history. Dark lines on the spectrum mark where certain very precise wavelengths are missing. These wavelengths were present when the light left the surface of the star, but were absorbed by atoms in the cooler, thinner gases of the star's atmosphere, above the surface. The dark absorption lines amount to a description of the star's atmosphere, of which hydrogen and helium are the main elements.

COSMIC FINGERPRINTS

As well as the marks of absorption, spectra also include so-called emission lines. These are peaks in brightness at very specific frequencies, which represent energy given off by a particular element. Like absorption lines, emission lines serve as cosmic fingerprints that identify the origins of the light beam that includes them.

Starlight also reveals the motion of its source. Light from a star that is moving toward the Earth will be blueshifted—that is, all the wavelengths in its light will be shortened slightly, so that a dark absorption line that normally shows in the yellow part of its spectrum appears toward the blue end. Light from a star that is moving away from the Earth is redshifted, so the same absorption line will be a corresponding distance toward the red.

The same effect gives clues to the temperature and density of a star's atmosphere. The denser the gas, the more atoms are present, and the higher the temperature, the faster the atoms are moving—in all directions. The result is a series of random red- and blueshifts. Absorption lines that are normally thin and sharp are stretched into thickened, fuzzy blurs.

Even after it has escaped into space, starlight is still gathering information. Clouds of gas and dust fill the spaces between the stars. The clouds are very sparse—far thinner than the best vacuum on Earth—but even so, the gas leaves telltale absorption lines in the starlight spectrum. Dust dims the starlight—around 40 percent might be lost over 1,500 light-years, and far more in dusty regions of the galaxy. The dust scatters shorter-wavelength blue light, whereas the longer reddish wavelengths pass freely. So red-tinged starlight may be from a star masked by light-years of dust.

REVEALING COLORS

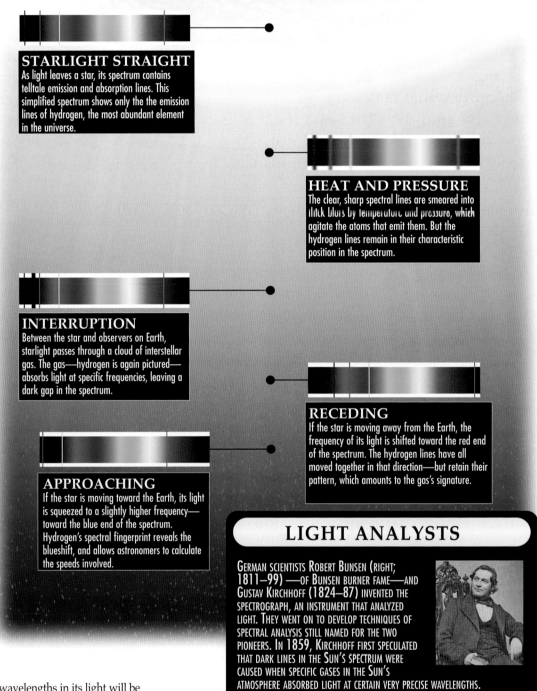

STARLIGHT STRAIGHT
As light leaves a star, its spectrum contains telltale emission and absorption lines. This simplified spectrum shows only the the emission lines of hydrogen, the most abundant element in the universe.

HEAT AND PRESSURE
The clear, sharp spectral lines are smeared into thick blurs by temperature and pressure, which agitate the atoms that emit them. But the hydrogen lines remain in their characteristic position in the spectrum.

INTERRUPTION
Between the star and observers on Earth, starlight passes through a cloud of interstellar gas. The gas—hydrogen is again pictured—absorbs light at specific frequencies, leaving a dark gap in the spectrum.

RECEDING
If the star is moving away from the Earth, the frequency of its light is shifted toward the red end of the spectrum. The hydrogen lines have all moved together in that direction—but retain their pattern, which amounts to the gas's signature.

APPROACHING
If the star is moving toward the Earth, its light is squeezed to a slightly higher frequency—toward the blue end of the spectrum. Hydrogen's spectral fingerprint reveals the blueshift, and allows astronomers to calculate the speeds involved.

LIGHT ANALYSTS

GERMAN SCIENTISTS ROBERT BUNSEN (RIGHT; 1811–99)—OF BUNSEN BURNER FAME—AND GUSTAV KIRCHHOFF (1824–87) INVENTED THE SPECTROGRAPH, AN INSTRUMENT THAT ANALYZED LIGHT. THEY WENT ON TO DEVELOP TECHNIQUES OF SPECTRAL ANALYSIS STILL NAMED FOR THE TWO PIONEERS. IN 1859, KIRCHHOFF FIRST SPECULATED THAT DARK LINES IN THE SUN'S SPECTRUM WERE CAUSED WHEN SPECIFIC GASES IN THE SUN'S ATMOSPHERE ABSORBED LIGHT AT CERTAIN VERY PRECISE WAVELENGTHS.

CLASSIFYING THE STARS

Faced with the chaos of five thousand visible stars, astronomers have always reacted by organizing. Ancient stargazers created the signs of the Zodiac. Modern astronomers can see many more stars and tell different stories from new groupings. Where the ancients painted heroes and animals on the sky, astronomers today turn starlight into science. "Classifying the stars is the greatest problem to be presented to the human mind," according to American astronomer Annie Jump Cannon. She should know—she has classified an incredible four hundred thousand of them in total.

STARS THAT DO NOT FIT

ASTRONOMERS CANNOT CLASSIFY EVERY STAR. THEY BRAND SOME ODDBALLS WITH A "P," FOR "PECULIAR."

NONSTANDARD STARS

VERY HOT WOLF-RAYET STARS HAVE PROBABLY LOST THEIR ATMOSPHERE. CARBON STARS ARE COOL AND RED AND FUSE ELEMENTS HEAVIER THAN HYDROGEN TO MAKE CARBON.

TECHNICALLY SPEAKING, SOME ARE NOT STARS AT ALL, SINCE THEIR CORES ARE TOO COLD TO BURN HYDROGEN: WHITE DWARFS' CORES ARE COLD BECAUSE THE STARS ARE TOO OLD; T-TAURI STARS ARE TOO YOUNG; BROWN DWARFS ARE TOO SMALL.

PLANETARY NEBULAE—ONCE CONFUSED WITH STARS—ARE ONLY STELLAR REMAINS. NOVAE ARE EXPLODING STARS.

WHERE ASTRONOMERS PUT THEM

ASTRONOMERS GIVE NEW CLASSIFICATION LETTERS TO SOME. WOLF-RAYET STARS HAVE BECOME GROUP "W," ABOVE "O." CARBON STARS BECOME THE "C" CLASSIFICATION, A HYBRID OF STARS IN GROUPS "K" AND "M." VERY COOL STARS ARE "L" AND "S." WHITE DWARFS' LETTER CLASSIFICATIONS ARE "DA," "DB," AND "DC."

STARS WITHOUT A LETTER CLASSIFICATION—T-TAURIS, FOR INSTANCE—CAN STILL BE PLOTTED ON A COLOR-LUMINOSITY GRAPH. THEY SIMPLY LIE AWAY FROM THE MAIN GROUPS OF STARS.

CHAOS TO CLARITY

To the untrained eye, stars all look similar. But the astronomers who assembled the famous Harvard University star catalog were eager to simplify and organize, and seized on small—but crucial—differences to tell them apart.

Their work—published mostly between 1918 and 1924—relied on an instrument called a spectrograph that splays visible light into a rainbow or spectrum of the light's component colors. But a spectrum of starlight contains more than a band of colors. It also has black lines crossing the band at particular points. These lines help astronomers work out what each star is made of.

To a scientist, the colors of the spectrum mean nothing more than electromagnetic radiation of specific wavelengths. The Danish physicist Niels Bohr (1885–1962) discovered that the dark and bright spectral lines are both created by the unique characteristics of atoms and molecules. If light travels through a substance, the electrons will absorb certain wavelengths, leaving gaps in a spectrum that show up as characteristic dark absorption lines. If a substance becomes hot enough to emit light, the electrons of its constituent atoms give off photons of light at those same wavelengths. An astrophysicist can measure these wavelengths by analyzing the light's spectrum and use them to identify the substances in a star.

Sometimes, though, the signature is unreadable. Above a certain temperature, atoms vibrate so much that they knock electrons out of orbit completely—so they do not absorb or emit any photons at all. Therefore, very hot stars often have weak spectral lines.

MULTIPLYING MESSAGES

Harvard astronomers first tried to classify the stars by spectral lines alone, but soon realized it would be more meaningful to classify them by temperature. Using a theory about energy emission by the German physicist Max Planck (1858–1947) with observations of starlight at different wavelengths, they could estimate a star's temperature from its color.

But as soon as they had begun reclassifying stars, another complication arose. Within a single temperature range, some stars had far thinner spectral lines. The astronomers realized that there was more data to be had from starlight. The width of the lines implied differences in size, density, and brightness as well.

In dense stars, atoms are relatively close together and so collide more frequently than the average. This has the effect of thickening spectral lines. Stars with narrow spectral lines are less dense but tend to be bigger. And given the same temperature, bigger stars are more luminous, since they have more surface area from which to radiate light.

In response to these insights, astronomers William Morgan and Philip Keenan devised a classification known for them as the "MK" system. It adds a scale of luminosity to the Harvard temperature scale so that astronomers can differentiate between stars with the same temperature—and therefore the same spectral class—but sometimes hugely different sizes, such as red dwarfs and red giants. The MK system uses five basic classes: supergiant, bright giant, giant, subgiant, and dwarf. In addition, the position of spectral lines yields information about the composition of a star, whether it is young and hydrogen-rich or old, riddled with heavy elements and perhaps likely to go supernova. With details of this kind, the data wrung out of a shaft of starlight can bring the mysterious points of light in the sky vividly to life.

FIRST LADY

PIONEER ASTRONOMER ANNIE JUMP CANNON SAW IT ALL. SHE SINGLE-HANDEDLY CLASSIFIED ALMOST EVERY ONE OF THE 225,000 STARS IN THE HARVARD COLLEGE OBSERVATORY STAR CATALOG.

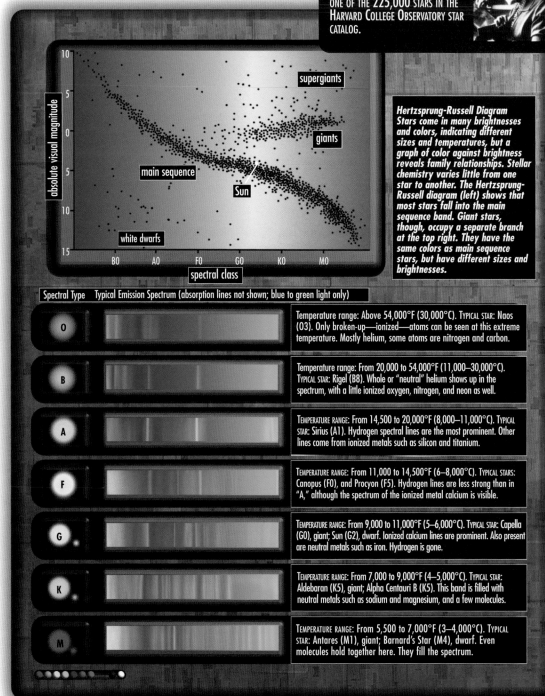

Hertzsprung-Russell Diagram
Stars come in many brightnesses and colors, indicating different sizes and temperatures, but a graph of color against brightness reveals family relationships. Stellar chemistry varies little from one star to another. The Hertzsprung-Russell diagram (left) shows that most stars fall into the main sequence band. Giant stars, though, occupy a separate branch at the top right. They have the same colors as main sequence stars, but have different sizes and brightnesses.

Spectral Type	Typical Emission Spectrum (absorption lines not shown; blue to green light only)	
O		Temperature range: Above 54,000°F (30,000°C). TYPICAL STAR: Naos (O3). Only broken-up—ionized—atoms can be seen at this extreme temperature. Mostly helium, some atoms are nitrogen and carbon.
B		Temperature range: From 20,000 to 54,000°F (11,000–30,000°C). TYPICAL STAR: Rigel (B8). Whole or "neutral" helium shows up in the spectrum, with a little ionized oxygen, nitrogen, and neon as well.
A		TEMPERATURE RANGE: From 14,500 to 20,000°F (8,000–11,000°C). TYPICAL STAR: Sirius (A1). Hydrogen spectral lines are the most prominent. Other lines come from ionized metals such as silicon and titanium.
F		TEMPERATURE RANGE: From 11,000 to 14,500°F (6–8,000°C). TYPICAL STARS: Canopus (F0), and Procyon (F5). Hydrogen lines are less strong than in "A," although the spectrum of the ionized metal calcium is visible.
G		TEMPERATURE RANGE: From 9,000 to 11,000°F (5–6,000°C). TYPICAL STAR: Capella (G0), giant; Sun (G2), dwarf. Ionized calcium lines are prominent. Also present are neutral metals such as iron. Hydrogen is gone.
K		TEMPERATURE RANGE: From 7,000 to 9,000°F (4–5,000°C). TYPICAL STAR: Aldebaran (K5), giant; Alpha Centauri B (K5). This band is filled with neutral metals such as sodium and magnesium, and a few molecules.
M		TEMPERATURE RANGE: From 5,500 to 7,000°F (3–4,000°C). TYPICAL STAR: Antares (M1), giant; Barnard's Star (M4), dwarf. Even molecules hold together here. They fill the spectrum.

THE COLOR OF STARS

Although almost all stars appear white to the naked eye, a closer look reveals that starlight is tinged with hues of red, orange, yellow, and blue. Astronomers have discovered that the distribution of these colors relates directly to the temperature at a star's surface. Cool ones are reddish, while those that are very hot appear a shade of light blue. And since a star's temperature reveals much about its composition, its age, and the workings of its core, the color of starlight has become a valuable long-distance tool for observing the universe and informing us about its stars.

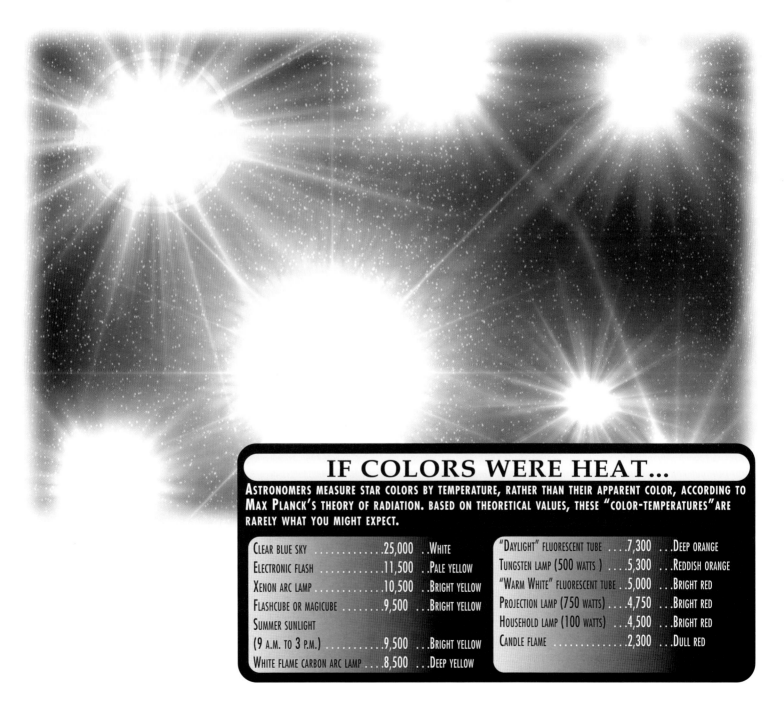

IF COLORS WERE HEAT...

ASTRONOMERS MEASURE STAR COLORS BY TEMPERATURE, RATHER THAN THEIR APPARENT COLOR, ACCORDING TO MAX PLANCK'S THEORY OF RADIATION. BASED ON THEORETICAL VALUES, THESE "COLOR-TEMPERATURES" ARE RARELY WHAT YOU MIGHT EXPECT.

CLEAR BLUE SKY	25,000	WHITE
ELECTRONIC FLASH	11,500	PALE YELLOW
XENON ARC LAMP	10,500	BRIGHT YELLOW
FLASHCUBE OR MAGICUBE	9,500	BRIGHT YELLOW
SUMMER SUNLIGHT (9 A.M. TO 3 P.M.)	9,500	BRIGHT YELLOW
WHITE FLAME CARBON ARC LAMP	8,500	DEEP YELLOW
"DAYLIGHT" FLUORESCENT TUBE	7,300	DEEP ORANGE
TUNGSTEN LAMP (500 WATTS)	5,300	REDDISH ORANGE
"WARM WHITE" FLUORESCENT TUBE	5,000	BRIGHT RED
PROJECTION LAMP (750 WATTS)	4,750	BRIGHT RED
HOUSEHOLD LAMP (100 WATTS)	4,500	BRIGHT RED
CANDLE FLAME	2,300	DULL RED

TRUE COLORS

Astronomers in the nineteenth century described star colors with equally colorful language. One 1887 book described the double stars of Beta Cygni as "yellow and sapphire blue" while those of Epsilon Boötis were apparently "pale orange and sea green." Clearly, describing and measuring star colors with the naked eye was an imprecise business.

Many of the star colors described by early stargazers are now thought to be false. For example, astronomers now believe that to the naked eye, green stars appear white—and that the "green" stars seen by nineteenth-century observers were optical illusions created by the color contrast between double stars. To guard against such mistakes, modern astronomy classifies the color of stars using a scientifically measured index. This is done by passing the starlight through filters that admit only certain wavelengths of light and then comparing the star's brightness as seen through each filter.

The reason for such painstaking work is that a star's true color reveals so much about its inner workings. In fact, analyzing the color of the light from a distant star yields far more information than a close-up black and white image of the same star ever could.

It was the German physicist Max Planck who first came up with the idea that a star's color could reveal its temperature. Planck's theory states that as the temperature of an object increases, so does the frequency of the radiation that it emits. For example, when a metal rod is heated, it begins by glowing red, then turns to orange, followed by white, and eventually blue. The same applies to stars: where the most light that is radiated from the star's surface falls in the visible spectrum bears a direct

relationship to its temperature—which can be anything between 3,000°F (1,650°C) and 360,000°F (200,000°C).

Planck's theory also explains why there are no green stars. A heated metal bar emits not just one frequency (and hence, color) of light, but a whole range. One way to imagine this is as a "hill" of radiation of different wavelengths in which the intensity falls away to either side of a "hilltop" that represents the dominant color.

Stars tend to be either reddish and bluish because these are the colors at the two ends of the visible

spectrum. When one or the other is dominant, there are relatively few other colors able to interfere with it. Green, by contrast, sits in the middle of the visible spectrum. So even when the temperature of a star makes green the dominant color, the many colors on either side of it tend to wash the green out, causing the star to appear white to the naked eye instead.

WHAT IF?

...WE FOUND A VIVID STAR?

Even the most vibrant stars in the universe are relatively washed-out. Although a reddish-looking star emits mostly red, orange, and yellow light, it also radiates light at all other frequencies in the visible spectrum that dilutes the colors.

It therefore would be a shock if an intensely colored jewel was discovered in the sky. The first reaction would be that it was not a star at all, but some kind of heavenly body—perhaps an undiscovered planet or unknown comet. The possibility that the object was an alien spacecraft would also be considered, since for a star to be a single color would overturn cosmological theory of the last 300 years. As far as we know, the core nuclear reactions that generate a star's radiation cannot produce light of just one frequency.

One possible explanation for such a vivid object is that it is a normal star surrounded by gas and dust that filters out all but a single frequency of its light. Different kinds of matter absorb wavelengths of radiation at different frequencies. So could a gas or dust cloud ever produce such an effect?

Although the idea is plausible, it is unlikely to occur in reality. Some of the most distant galaxies are quasars, whose radiation travels billions of light-years to reach us. Even though this radiation passes through many thousands of galaxies on its way to Earth, it remains largely intact. Therefore, it is almost unthinkable that the elements needed to absorb so many frequencies of radiation would be present in the same place along the path of just one electromagnetic wave.

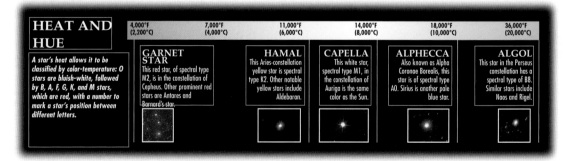

HEAT AND HUE

A star's heat allows it to be classified by color-temperature: O stars are bluish-white, followed by B, A, F, G, K, and M stars, which are red, with a number to mark a star's position between different letters.

	4,000°F (2,200°C)	7,000°F (4,000°C)	11,000°F (6,000°C)	14,000°F (8,000°C)	18,000°F (10,000°C)	36,000°F (20,000°C)
	GARNET STAR This red star, of spectral type M2, is in the constellation of Cepheus. Other prominent red stars are Antares and Barnard's star.	**HAMAL** This Aries-constellation yellow star is spectral type K2. Other notable yellow stars include Aldebaran.	**CAPELLA** This white star, spectral type M1, in the constellation of Auriga is the same color as the Sun.	**ALPHECCA** Also known as Alpha Coronae Borealis, this star is of spectral type A0. Sirius is another pale blue star.	**ALGOL** This star in the Perseus constellation has a spectral type of B8. Similar stars include Naos and Rigel.

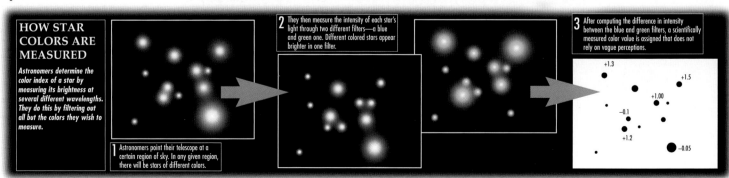

HOW STAR COLORS ARE MEASURED

Astronomers determine the color index of a star by measuring its brightness at several different wavelengths. They do this by filtering out all but the colors they wish to measure.

1 Astronomers point their telescope at a certain region of sky. In any given region, there will be stars of different colors.

2 They then measure the intensity of each star's light through two different filters—a blue and green one. Different colored stars appear brighter in one filter.

3 After computing the difference in intensity between the blue and green filters, a scientifically measured color value is assigned that does not rely on vague perceptions.

+1.3
+1.5
+1.00
−0.1
+1.2
−0.05

STAR DISTANCES

How do you find the distance to an unreachable star? Even the nearest stars are so remote that they appear only as pinpoints of light, and there is no immediate hope of traveling to them, let alone of stretching some hypothetical tape measure all the way out there. Yet astronomers speak confidently of the distances of stars thousands of light-years away. The method they use is simple in principle, and recent measurements from space using the Hipparcos satellite have improved its accuracy.

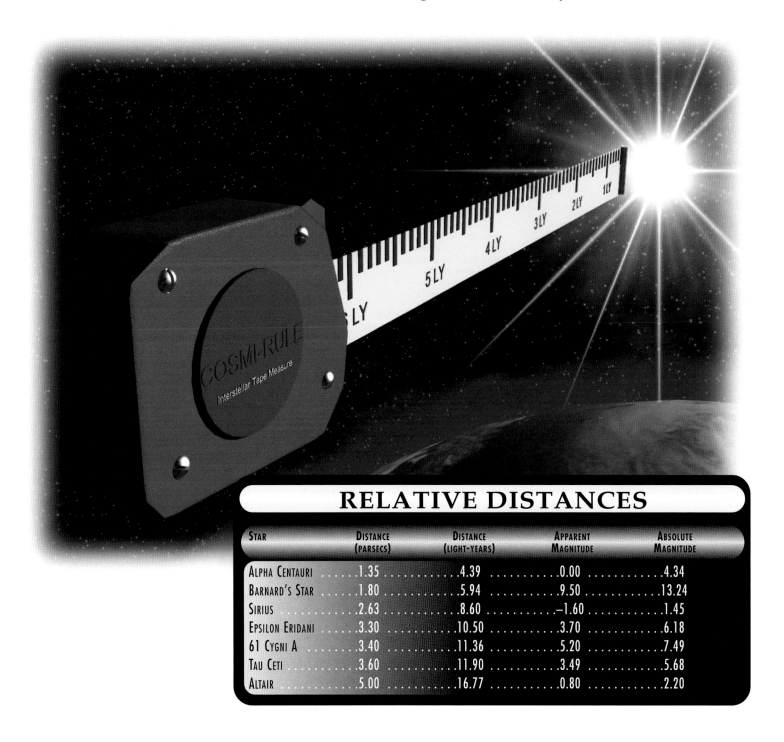

RELATIVE DISTANCES

Star	Distance (parsecs)	Distance (light-years)	Apparent Magnitude	Absolute Magnitude
Alpha Centauri	1.35	4.39	0.00	4.34
Barnard's Star	1.80	5.94	9.50	13.24
Sirius	2.63	8.60	−1.60	1.45
Epsilon Eridani	3.30	10.50	3.70	6.18
61 Cygni A	3.40	11.36	5.20	7.49
Tau Ceti	3.60	11.90	3.49	5.68
Altair	5.00	16.77	0.80	2.20

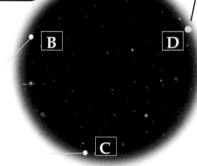

...AND THE UNKNOWN
A more distant star, D, with a similar spectrum to A, will be of the same type and therefore the same true brightness. Astronomers compare its apparent brightness with that of A to estimate its distance.

NEAR MISS

THE FIRST STAR DISTANCE (FOUR LIGHT-YEARS TO ALPHA CENTAURI) WAS MEASURED IN 1833 BY THOMAS HENDERSON (RIGHT) IN SOUTH AFRICA. BUT HE SAT ON THE RESULTS FOR SIX YEARS, SO THE CREDIT FOR THE FIRST MEASUREMENT WENT TO GERMAN ASTRONOMER F.W. BESSEL, WHO PUBLISHED THE DISTANCE TO 61 CYGNI IN 1838.

VIEW FROM Y
From this side of Earth's orbit, star A appears closer to star B. In practice, the shift in position is minute.

VIEW FROM X
From one side of the Earth's orbit, nearby star A appears to be closer to star C than to star B.

THE KNOWN...
A star's spectrum shows dark lines caused by material in the star's atmosphere. Each type of star has characteristic lines. Since the distance to star A has been measured directly, astronomers can calculate its true brightness.

A

GETTING FROM A TO D

SUN

The distance of star A can be measured from Earth using the parallax method, based on its apparent shift in position relative to B and C when viewed from X and Y. Once the much more distant star D is identified as having a similar spectrum to A, its distance can be estimated based on its apparent brightness.

HIPPARCOS

THE HIPPARCOS SATELLITE, DESIGNED TO MEASURE STAR DISTANCES ACCURATELY, WAS ALMOST A FLOP. A FAULTY ROCKET LEFT THE SPACECRAFT IN A HIGHLY ELLIPTICAL ORBIT THAT PASSED THROUGH THE VAN ALLEN BELTS OF RADIATION AROUND THE EARTH. BUT THE SATELLITE SURVIVED AND THE MISSION WAS REPLANNED TO ALLOW FOR THE NEW ORBIT.

HOW FAR'S THAT STAR?

The system that astronomers use to measure star distances is little more than an extension of the way we judge distances with our eyes—the method of parallax. Each eye sees from a slightly different viewpoint, and our brains use the difference to gauge distances to nearby objects. For a more distant object, such as a far-off mountain peak, the few inches between our eyes are not enough. So mapmakers often begin their work by pacing out a baseline, after which they can measure the angles from the ends of the baseline to their target object and work out the object's distance using the branch of math known as trigonometry.

The stars are so far off that astronomers need the longest baseline they can possibly find—

the orbit of the Earth around the Sun. This allows them to make measurements, six months apart, that are separated by 186 million miles (300 million km). The parallax—which is the shift in the star's apparent position when viewed from these two points—reveals its distance.

For example, the nearest bright star—Alpha Centauri—shifts only about 1.5 arc seconds as seen from either side of the Earth's orbit. Though the angle is tiny—equivalent to the gap between a car's headlights in Philadelphia as seen from New York City—in the case of Alpha Centauri, it translates as a distance of 26 trillion miles (42 trillion km). Because such large numbers rapidly become unmanageable, astronomers have their own units of measurement for star distances. Professional astronomers use parsecs, that is, the distance that a

star would have to be for its angle of parallax (as measured across the 93-million-mile (150m km) radius of the Earth's orbit) to be exactly one arc second. Expressed in these units, Alpha Centauri is 1.347 parsecs from Earth.

Many people prefer to think of interstellar distances in terms of the time light would take to reach us from the star. Light travels at 186,000 miles (300,000 km) per second, and in a year it covers about 6 trillion miles (9.7 trillion km)—or one light-year. There are 3.26 light-years in a parsec. Most stars that are visible to the naked eye are within a few hundred light-years.

BREAKING THE BLUR BARRIER

Star parallaxes are complicated by the fact that stars are not stationary but moving through space. It takes several years of measurement to disentangle a star's parallax from its proper motion. The Earth's turbulent atmosphere, which blurs star

images, is another barrier to accurate measurement. In fact, only about 100 stars are close enough for their distances to be measured by parallax from Earth-based telescopes.

Greater accuracy is possible from space, which is why the Hipparcos satellite was launched in 1989. As a result, the distances of over 7,000 stars are now known within 5 percent. But although Hipparcos can provide reliable data within 500 light-years of the Earth, the number of stars whose parallax can be measured directly is a tiny proportion of the total number of stars in our galaxy.

In the case of more distant stars, astronomers use a less accurate method. First they compare the star's brightness and spectrum—its signature—with those of nearby stars whose distance is known. Astronomers then assume that two stars with similar spectra will be of similar true brightness, which allows them to place the more distant of the two stars by measuring the apparent difference in brightness between them.

WEIGHING STARS

Astronomers have a scale that can weigh the stars: gravity. Their technique relies on very precise observations that measure how much the gravitational pull of one star affects a near companion and, hence, just how much mass has done the pulling. Such observations give accurate data for only a few dozen stars. But because astronomers know how mass is linked to brightness, they can estimate the mass of many more stars—and learn more about how they live and die.

RELATIVE STAR WEIGHTS

STAR	MASS (SUN = 1)	LUMINOSITY (SUN = 1)	DIAMETER (SUN = 1)	DIAMETER (MILES/KM)
UV CETI B	0.035	0.00004	UNKNOWN	UNKNOWN
UV CETI A	0.044	0.00006	UNKNOWN	UNKNOWN
ROSS 614 B	0.08	0.00003	UNKNOWN	UNKNOWN
PROXIMA CENTAURI	0.1	0.00005	UNKNOWN	UNKNOWN
61 CYGNI A	0.63	0.08	UNKNOWN	UNKNOWN
ETA CASSIOPEIAE	0.85	1.24	0.84	727,000/1.16M
ALPHA CENTAURI B	0.89	0.45	0.87	753,000/1,21M
SIRIUS B	0.98	0.002	0.02	20,000/32,000
ALPHA CENTAURI A	1.1	1.6	1.2	1,100,000/1.7M
SIRIUS	2.31	23.1	1.8	1,560,000/2.5M

GRAVITY'S SCALES

How on Earth do you weigh a star? The answer is surprisingly simple. You use the same universal force of gravity that allows you to weigh things on Earth. When you stand on a bathroom scale, the scale measures the tug of gravity—and displays your weight. The same force of gravity holds the Earth in its orbit around the Sun and grips every star in every galaxy throughout the universe.

The first star anyone weighed was the Sun, which involved a relatively straightforward procedure. The distance from the Earth to the Sun was known, as was the length of the Earth's orbital period of exactly one year. The equations of orbits and gravity worked out by Johannes Kepler and Sir Isaac Newton back in the seventeenth century did the rest. Calculation showed the Sun was 333,000 times the mass of the Earth.

Unfortunately, other stars are far too distant from Earth to have any measurable gravitational effect. But the stars are not necessarily distant from each other. Unlike the Sun, most of the galaxy's stars are binaries, pairs of stars that orbit each other around a common center of mass. If astronomers can find a binary's orbital period and measure the distance that separates the two stars, they can use gravitational equations to calculate the combined mass of the pair.

SEEING THE LIGHT

Some nearby binary stars show clearly in telescopes. They can be seen orbiting each other, taking from days to years to do so. In these cases, astronomers can find the masses of the stars using the same equations that they use to find the Sun's weight. The masses of about 50 binary stars can be found by this method. But for other binary stars, too distant to be made out individually, astronomers use the techniques of spectroscopy. Spectroscopy involves splitting a star's light into a rainbow of color, or a spectrum. Within the rainbow are thin lines that correspond to gases in the star's atmosphere, which absorb light at a very specific frequency and leave a dark gap in the spectrum. The exact position of the lines shows whether a star is moving toward or away from Earth. If receding, the spectral lines move toward the red

end of the spectrum. If it is approaching, they move toward the blue.

For a pair of stars, the lines from them are seen to separate each time one star is moving toward us and one is moving away. Regular observations yield both the period of rotation and the speeds of the stars. After making an assumption about whether the stars are more or less edge-on or face-on, astronomers can feed the data into the equations and get values for the star's masses.

Using information gleaned from well-observed double stars, astronomers can link the mass of a star with many of its other properties, especially its true brightness. Given a star's spectrum and brightness, they can confidently assign it a mass—which means that they can now estimate the masses of most of the stars they can see in the sky. Even so, most of our knowledge of star masses is still based on precise observations of just 50 stars that are near to us.

HARD EVIDENCE

SPECTRAL CLUES
Both light waves and sound waves are affected by the movement of their source. In the case of sound waves, the shift is audible—as in the change of note of a car as it races past you. Light changes wavelength, which shows up in its spectrum. At left are two spectra of a faint binary star, taken at different times. The dark lines, which indicate silicon in the primary star, show up clearly. In the top picture, the fainter or secondary star of the pair was moving toward us, so its silicon lines are to the left of the main lines (blueshifted). On the lower picture the star was moving away, so its spectral lines have slipped to the right of those of the primary star (redshifted).

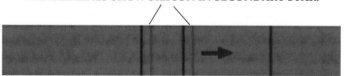

DARKER LINES INDICATE SILICON IN PRIMARY STAR.

FAINTER LINES SHOW SILICON IN SECONDARY STAR.

BINARY IN BALANCE

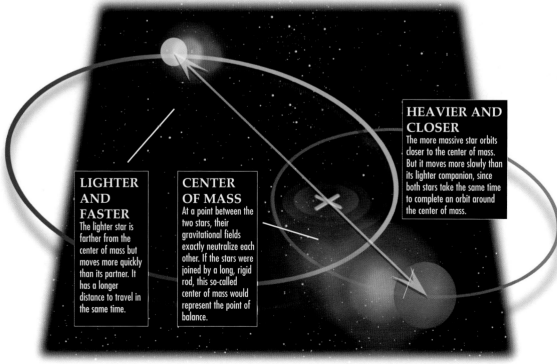

LIGHTER AND FASTER
The lighter star is farther from the center of mass but moves more quickly than its partner. It has a longer distance to travel in the same time.

CENTER OF MASS
At a point between the two stars, their gravitational fields exactly neutralize each other. If the stars were joined by a long, rigid rod, this so-called center of mass would represent the point of balance.

HEAVIER AND CLOSER
The more massive star orbits closer to the center of mass. But it moves more slowly than its lighter companion, since both stars take the same time to complete an orbit around the center of mass.

HARD EVIDENCE

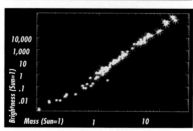

HEAVIER MEANS BRIGHTER
Once astronomers weighed enough stars to have a good range of stellar masses on record, they compared mass against luminosity—the amount of light a star gives out. They found that light output increases dramatically with mass. A star 10 times heavier than the Sun, for example, is 10,000 times brighter. The link between mass and brightness is consistent for most stars. So if they know a star's distance, astronomers work out its real brightness from its apparent brightness. Then they use a version of the graph shown above to find the star's mass—even if they cannot weigh it by other means.

STELLAR LIFE CYCLES

All stars begin life in a similar way, as clouds of gas and dust collapsing and condensing under their own gravity to form protostars. The exact conditions within the protostellar nebula, however, are key to the star's later life story. Some stars are able to grow unfettered, pulling in enormous amounts of material and reaching many times the mass of the Sun. Some have their supply of material cut off when they are still small, and form dwarf stars far fainter than the Sun. Eventually, all stars reach an equilibrium in which they spend most of their lives, converting hydrogen to helium in fusion reactions at their core. But as the core fuel supply runs out, the differences between stellar life stories becomes more marked. Stars like the Sun end their lives in a relatively sedate way, ballooning to form red giants and then shedding their outer layers as beautiful planetary nebulae, but the most massive stars are destroyed in spectacular supernova explosions. This process forms stellar remnants—among some of the strangest objects in the universe.

BIRTH OF
A STAR

The birth of a star takes much too long for any one person to witness, although on a cosmic timescale it is a relatively rapid process—it "only" takes millions of years. The process begins when a vast expanse of gas and dust known as a "dark cloud" begins to contract and heat up, causing the center of the cloud to become so dense and hot that it then blows away the surrounding layers. Then what remains of the cloud contracts still further, triggering the nuclear fusion reactions that cause a new star to begin to shine in the night sky.

SITES OF STAR FORMATION

NAME	DISTANCE (LIGHT-YEARS)	CONSTELLATION
ORION NEBULA	1,500	ORION
OMEGA NEBULA	5,000	SAGITTARIUS
LAGOON NEBULA	5,200	SAGITTARIUS
TRIFID NEBULA	5,200	SAGITTARIUS
EAGLE NEBULA	7,000	SERPENS

A STAR IS BORN

Astar begins its life as a cold, dark cloud of gas and dust that begins to contract and collapse in on itself. But scientists still cannot say for certain under what conditions this process is triggered. One cause seems to be the gravitational pulls of neighboring stars in the galaxy, which at times may squeeze and stretch a dark cloud. Another trigger could be shock waves—either from other stars in the process of forming, or from giant stars that have recently "died" in supernova explosions. This would explain why star formation appears to have a snowball effect and why new stars often emerge in clusters.

Eventually a dark cloud contracts to the point where it starts to collapse under its own weight. As it does, it gets denser, and the resulting friction generates heat in increasingly vast amounts.

PROTOSTAR

At this point the temperature rises rapidly and the cloud becomes what astronomers call a protostar— a "potential" star. Although shrouded in dust and gas, it is a big source of infrared radiation. As the temperature at the core of a protostar reaches around 20 million °F (11 million °C), a nuclear fusion reaction begins in which hydrogen atoms in the core turn into helium atoms, giving off energy as they do so. The protostar flares up to become a full-fledged star. A violent "stellar wind" blows away the remaining outer layers of gas and dust, giving rise to jet flows that can be seen over great distances. In the case of a star measuring the approximate size of our Sun, the birth process takes around 50 million years. Within the star's interior, the inward pull of gravity is precisely balanced by the outward flow of energy, and the star settles down to a lifetime of steady burning that lasts billions of years.

STAR CHILD

EACH OF US CAN TRULY BE CALLED A STAR CHILD, MADE OUT OF STARDUST. ALL THE ATOMS IN OUR BODIES, EXCEPT FOR HYDROGEN, WERE FORGED IN DISTANT STARS LONG BEFORE OUR SOLAR SYSTEM WAS BORN.

FOUR STAGES OF STAR FORMATION

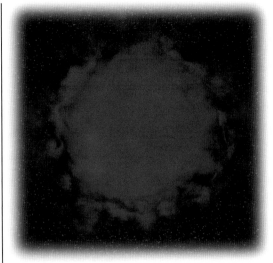

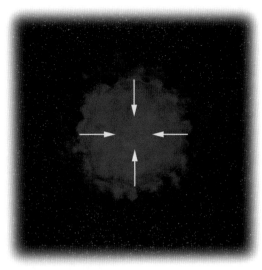

1 TRIGGER
Star formation begins when a dark cloud of dust and gas is disturbed by outside pressures and begins to collapse in on itself. Such disturbances may result from gravitational forces met while passing through a spiral galaxy. They may also be due to cosmic shock waves—such as those from other newly formed stars, or from giant stars that "die" in a supernova explosion, such as SN 1987A (left), first seen in 1987.

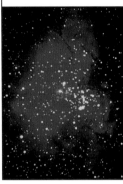

2 COLLAPSE
Once the collapse of a dark cloud has been triggered, it continues under its own momentum. Gravity forces draw the dust particles and gas molecules toward the core at an ever increasing rate. It was by this process that the Eagle nebula (left) in the constellation of Serpens—which is 7,000 light-years from Earth—changed from an invisible interstellar dust cloud into a bright and active region of star formation.

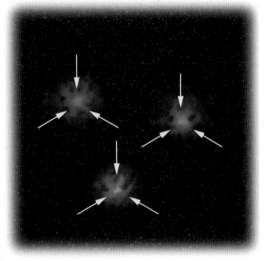

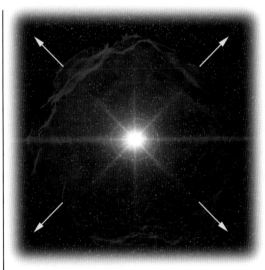

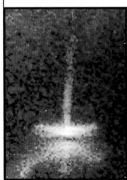

3 SMALL CLOUDS
As the collapsing cloud contracts, it heats up and becomes what is known as a protostar. The temperature climbs to millions of degrees, then nuclear fusion reactions begin and the star flares into life. A forceful "stellar wind" sweeps away the surrounding material and lights up nearby gas clouds. Sometimes the "stellar wind" is channeled into jets of gas known as Herbig-Haro jets.

4 NEW STAR
After the gas streams expelled by the newborn star have blasted away the surrounding gas and dust, the star finally emerges from its nursery. New stars often form in clusters such as the Trapezium group (left) in the Orion nebula. The majority of stars are not single, but have one or more other stars in orbit around them. The Sun is unusual in not having such a companion.

BROWN DWARFS

Brown dwarfs are stars that never quite made the grade. By planetary standards, they are immense—up to eighty times the size of Jupiter—but even this incredible size is not massive enough to sustain the nuclear fusion reactions that burn at the heart of real stars. These stellar failures glow so dimly that astronomers have only recently been able to detect them. Yet brown dwarfs may represent a missing link in theories of star and planet formation. Though hard to see, they could be more numerous than the stars themselves.

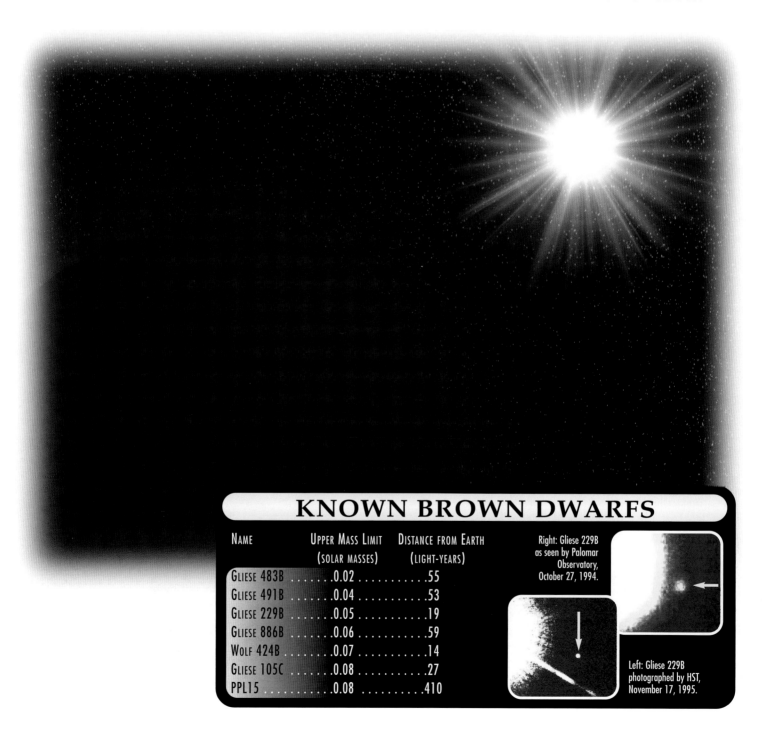

KNOWN BROWN DWARFS

Name	Upper Mass Limit (solar masses)	Distance from Earth (light-years)
Gliese 483B	0.02	55
Gliese 491B	0.04	53
Gliese 229B	0.05	19
Gliese 886B	0.06	59
Wolf 424B	0.07	14
Gliese 105C	0.08	27
PPL15	0.08	410

Right: Gliese 229B as seen by Palomar Observatory, October 27, 1994.

Left: Gliese 229B photographed by HST, November 17, 1995.

FAILED STARS

A brown dwarf begins life in the same way as all successful stars—as a lump of matter condensing from a swirling cloud of hydrogen. But its birth cloud is too small, and the brown dwarf never quite makes the grade.

Regular stars come in all sizes, from red dwarfs that are half the radius of the Sun to supergiants a thousand times larger. All of these bodies, though, have at least several hundred times more mass than even the heaviest known planets, and it is this mass that turns them into stars. Under the crushing pressure at the core, temperatures rise above 5 million°F (2.7 million °C)—enough to fuse the hydrogen atoms into helium. The energy released in this process not only makes the star shine brightly, but creates an outward gas pressure that balances the inward pull of gravity and holds the star together.

If a star in the process of forming cannot amass sufficient bulk—about 8 percent of the mass of the Sun—its core never reaches the critical fusion temperature and it becomes a brown dwarf instead. With no internal energy source to balance its gravity, the failed star slowly collapses inward. The collapse itself generates some heat and the brown dwarf shines after a fashion—but less brightly and for less time than even the faintest fusion-powered star.

Compared with most real stars, the active life of a brown dwarf is short. Its only heat source is the energy released by shrinking under its own gravity, and after a few hundred million years the dwarf's core becomes so dense that even gravity cannot compress it any further. At this point, the brown dwarf—by now crushed to perhaps half of its initial diameter—quietly peters out. Very slowly its residual heat leaks away into space and it begins to fade into darkness.

DIM RED LIGHT

Despite their name, brown dwarfs are not actually brown. A brown dwarf with 5 percent of the Sun's mass, for example, would have a surface temperature of around 4,000°F (2,200°C), causing it to glow deep red. But in appearance, such an object would be hard to tell apart from a far-off red dwarf, the smallest of the true stars.

Because brown dwarfs are so cool by stellar standards, most of their energy is infrared. So although astronomers predicted their existence as far back as 1963, they had to wait for 1990s equipment, including space-based infrared telescopes, before they could be observed. The first brown dwarf was detected in 1994, 19 light-years away in the Lepus constellation. Astronomers now think that brown dwarfs may be more common than stars in our galaxy—but we may only ever see the brightest and the nearest ones.

DULL COMPANION

THE FIRST BROWN DWARF EVER OBSERVED—SHOWN AT RIGHT IN THE CENTER OF A HUBBLE SPACE TELESCOPE IMAGE—IS KNOWN ONLY BY ITS CATALOG NAME OF GLIESE 229B. THE OBJECT HAS ABOUT THE SAME DIAMETER AS JUPITER, BUT HAS 50 TIMES MORE MASS. THE SURFACE TEMPERATURE IS 1,300°F (700°C), COMPARED WITH THE 9,750°F (5,400°C) OF OUR OWN SUN. GLIESE 229B ORBITS A FAINT RED DWARF JUST 19 LIGHT-YEARS FROM EARTH, IN THE CONSTELLATION LEPUS. IT WAS DISCOVERED IN 1994.

PLEIADES DWARF

THE PLEIADES IS A CLUSTER OF YOUNG STARS SOME 410 LIGHT-YEARS AWAY THAT MAY HARBOR SEVERAL BROWN DWARFS. ONE OBJECT, CALLED PPL15, HAS ONLY 6 TO 8 PERCENT OF THE SUN'S MASS. IN 1996, ASTRONOMERS DISCOVERED THAT ITS LIGHT SPECTRUM CONTAINS LITHIUM, AN ELEMENT THAT IS USUALLY DESTROYED BY ATMOSPHERIC HEAT IN REGULAR STARS.

BRIGHT STARS, BROWN EMBERS

NUCLEAR FURNACE
At the core of a regular star, the star's gravity creates pressure and temperatures so high that thermonuclear fusion reactions begin. The pressure of the energy released by these reactions is enough to hold off further gravitational collapse.

GRAVITY SQUEEZE
The gravity of a brown dwarf causes a slow collapse that generates enough heat for the dwarf to glow. But there is never enough heat or pressure to trigger star-like thermonuclear activity.

DENSE CORE
The gravitational collapse eventually creates a core of superdense "degenerate" matter that resists further compression. Deprived of the heat caused by shrinkage, the brown dwarf slowly begins to cool.

STAR

BROWN DWARF

THE MAIN SEQUENCE

When stars are plotted according to their color (temperature) and brightness (absolute magnitude) on a graph known as a Hertzsprung-Russell diagram, the vast majority of them show up as a curving diagonal band that astronomers refer to as the main sequence. Such stars are all in the stable, middle-aged phase of their long lives. These stars neither expand nor contract, and they consistently convert hydrogen into helium at a steady rate. The Sun is safely on the main sequence—otherwise, life on Earth would be impossible—and so are about 90 percent of the stars in the universe.

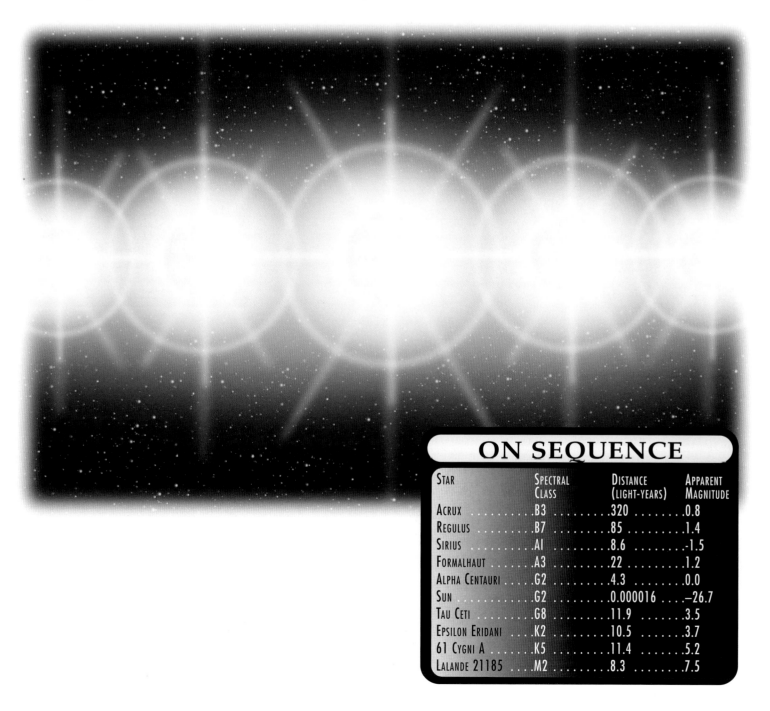

ON SEQUENCE

Star	Spectral Class	Distance (light-years)	Apparent Magnitude
Acrux	B3	320	0.8
Regulus	B7	85	1.4
Sirius	A1	8.6	-1.5
Formalhaut	A3	22	1.2
Alpha Centauri	G2	4.3	0.0
Sun	G2	0.000016	—26.7
Tau Ceti	G8	11.9	3.5
Epsilon Eridani	K2	10.5	3.7
61 Cygni A	K5	11.4	5.2
Lalande 21185	M2	8.3	7.5

GOING STEADY

A star is born in the whirl of a collapsing cloud of gas. When pressures and temperatures at the star's core rise high enough, nuclear fusion begins. Hydrogen—which makes up around 75 percent of most new stars—is converted into helium at a remarkably steady rate. The star shines, and the radiation pressure from its nuclear-burning heart keeps it from collapsing under its own gravity.

Once those hydrogen fires have ignited, the star begins its career on what astronomers call the main sequence. So long as there is hydrogen to burn, the star will remain there. And how long that will be depends on just one thing: the star's mass. Massive stars burn their fuel quickly, and glow brightly. Because of their high surface temperatures, their light is blue. Within a few million years, their hydrogen is gone, and they move out of the main sequence into the next stage of their evolution. Low-mass stars burn slowly. Much cooler than the blue giants, they glow a dim red. But they keep on glowing for many billions of years.

There are top and bottom limits at each end of the main sequence scale. Stars larger than 60 times the mass of the Sun are unstable—they blow themselves apart before their main sequence life can begin. And stars with less than 8 percent of the Sun's mass never become hot enough at their cores for hydrogen fusion to start. In between those limits, main sequence stars can range from ferociously hot blue giants down to dim red dwarfs.

GRAPHIC UNDERSTANDING

Early in the twentieth century, astronomers Ejnar Hertzsprung and Henry Norris Russell discovered an interesting pattern. When they plotted the temperatures of stars—in effect, their colors—against their luminosity, the resulting graph showed that 90 percent of them fell into a diagonal line from the top left to the bottom right. This so-called Hertzsprung-Russell (HR) diagram turned out to be a great step forward in understanding the stars.

The stars at the top left are hot, blue, big, and young. Those at the bottom right are cool, red, small, and old—possibly almost as old as the universe. Somewhere in between lies our own Sun, technically a yellow dwarf star

with a main sequence life of around 9 billion years, half of which still remains before it.

The HR diagram also tells much about the remaining 10 percent of stars—those not on the main sequence. As stars age, they drift gently across the diagram. The Sun, for example, will eventually consume its hydrogen. It will cool down, but also

expand greatly in size. So it will become redder and more luminous, and its HR position will move upward and to the right. Later, its fires will dim as it shrugs off its outward layers. As a white dwarf, the Sun will sink toward the bottom left of the HR diagram. It will still glow dimly—because it is hot—but its nuclear furnaces will be extinct.

HARD EVIDENCE

QUICK COUNT

The mass of a star determines how much fuel it contains and how fast the star will burn it, so there is a simple relationship between mass and lifetime on the main sequence. Astronomers usually calculate this by comparing the mass of the star in question with that of the Sun. A star 10 times as massive as the Sun, for example, will spend just 100 million years on the main sequence. A small star of 0.1 solar masses—Gliese 623B is shown here—may stay there for a trillion years.

MIDDLE-AGE SPREAD

On a graph that plots the surface temperature of stars against their luminosity, most appear in a diagonal line called the main sequence: they are quietly getting on with their adult lives.

The luminosity axis on this Hertzsprung-Russell diagram shows the real brightness of stars on a scale where the Sun measures 1. The temperature—which dictates a star's color—is measured in degrees Kelvin above absolute zero. The Sun is a G-type star.

Luminosity axis values: 10^6, 10^4, 10^2, 1, 10^{-2}, 10^{-4}

Temperature (K): 40,000 20,000 10,000 7500 5500 4500 3000

Absolute Magnitude: -10, -5, 0, 5, 10, 15

Spectral Class: O B A F G K M

HOT BLUE

Blue giant stars in the constellation of Orion blaze furiously. But within 100 million years they will be extinct—blasted off the main sequence by the supernova explosions that will destroy them.

YELLOW DWARF

The Sun is technically a yellow dwarf, although as this true color picture shows, our nearest star is actually white. It should remain on the main sequence for another 5 billion years.

DIM RED

The red dwarf star Gliese 105 and its tiny companion star consume fuel so slowly that they will stay on the main sequence for billions of years. They may already be more than 10 billion years old.

RED GIANTS

When a star has exhausted its store of hydrogen fuel, it does not simply fizzle out. Instead, the star's core collapses and its outer layers begin to expand enormously. The result, at least for a time, is the large, luminous but relatively cool star known as a red giant. Although red giants eventually go on to die in different ways—the exact circumstances depend on their mass and chemical composition—all stars will eventually pass through the red giant stage, including our own Sun.

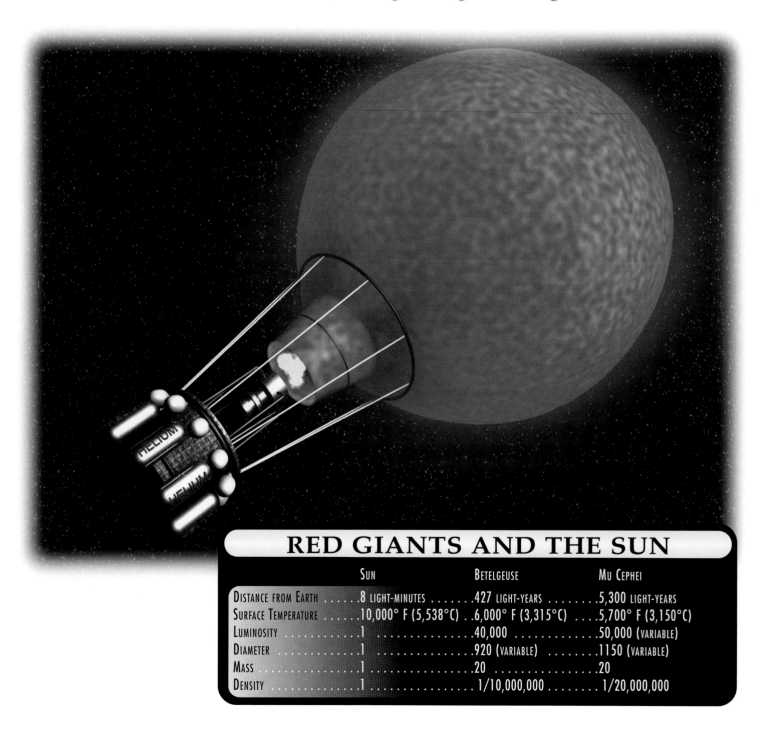

RED GIANTS AND THE SUN

	Sun	Betelgeuse	Mu Cephei
Distance from Earth	.8 light-minutes	.427 light-years	.5,300 light-years
Surface Temperature	10,000° F (5,538°C)	.6,000° F (3,315°C)	.5,700° F (3,150°C)
Luminosity	1	40,000	50,000 (variable)
Diameter	1	.920 (variable)	.1150 (variable)
Mass	1	.20	.20
Density	1	1/10,000,000	1/20,000,000

SWOLLEN STARS

Most stars are so far away that even the largest telescope shows them only as a point of light. But a few stars are so big that careful observations from Earth reveal their true disks despite their distance. These are the red giants. They are not especially massive—their mass may be similar to the Sun's—but they are so swollen that the whole of the Earth's orbit could fit inside one. Yet red giants are no stellar freaks. Once, they were typical stars, producing a steady stream of energy. Now, they are nearing the end of their lives.

When a star has burned most of its hydrogen fuel, the core of helium "ash" collapses under its own weight. The star contracts by 98 percent and compression makes it heat up until hydrogen starts burning to helium in a thin shell around the core. As the zone of hydrogen fusion migrates away from the center, the core grows denser and hotter until eventually its energy sends the star's outer layers billowing into space. In only a few hundred million years, the star's diameter increases by more than a hundredfold, cooling to about half its previous temperature.

The temperature drop means that the star's light becomes much redder, like the cooling embers of a fire. But the vast increase in the star's surface area ensures that the actual energy output is now much greater than before. Red giant stars are among the most luminous that can be seen in the sky.

Meanwhile, the core continues to contract until the helium is so tightly compressed that its nuclei and electrons are crushed together. Eventually, the core reaches a temperature high enough to fuse the helium to carbon, but because the core material is so densely packed, it behaves more like molten metal than a gas. Instead of expanding, it simply gets hotter. Fusion accelerates until, at a temperature of 180,000,000° F (100,000,000°C), the core abruptly reverts to a gas and explodes.

But when the central helium fuel runs out, the core collapses again. This time, energy generated swells the star into a red supergiant so spread out that gravity has only a tenuous hold on its outer layers.

At this stage many supergiants begin to pulsate, as violent core explosions alternate with cooling and contraction. The precise behavior of each star depends on its mass. Huge stars, such as Betelgeuse in the constellation of Orion, may flicker erratically. Lighter stars, such as Mira in Cetus, can cycle from bright to faint over a period of months. For the lighter stars, helium is the last usable power source. Eventually nuclear burning will cease. The star will throw off its outer layers to become a planetary nebula. More massive stars may end their lives more spectacularly in the dramatic explosions known as supernovae.

AILING GIANTS

STEADY BURN
For most of its life, a star converts hydrogen to helium in its core (blue). Outward pressure from nuclear fusion balances the force of gravity that pulls inward. This "main sequence" lasts for about 10 billion years.

EXPANSION
After all the available hydrogen has been consumed, nuclear fusion ends and the star collapses under its own weight. As the core contracts, the outer layers expand and cool, radiating red light. This stage may last for a few hundred million years.

HELIUM FLASH
The helium core—heated to 180 million°F (100 million°C)—explodes, and thrusts the star's outer clouds farther. The explosion ignites two separate nuclear fires: in the inner core (blue) helium fuses into carbon, and in the cooler middle shell, hydrogen is fused into helium. Depending on the star's mass, it may only have a few thousand years left to live.

LONG SHOT

In 1933, the organizers of the second Great Exposition in Chicago had a bright idea. To mark the 40 years since the previous Exposition, they used rays from the red giant Arcturus—thought to be 40 light-years away—to turn on the lights. They collected starlight with a telescope and focused it on a newfangled photocell switch. It worked. Sadly, according to later measurements, Arcturus is 37 light-years away.

A CENTURY OF PROGRESS
1833   1933
COME! CHICAGO WORLD'S FAIR

BLUE SUPERGIANTS

Hotter than any other stars, blue supergiants are the most powerful stars known. These stellar monsters are at least ten to twenty times the diameter of the Sun, as well as being much brighter, and some emit more energy than hundreds of thousands of smaller, normal stars. In some cases, the radiation emitted by these stars is powerful enough to take some of a blue supergiant's outer layers with it, to form a vast gaseous envelope around the giant star. As a result of such fierce activity, these stars have some of the shortest known stellar lives—lasting only a million years or so.

SOME BLUE SUPERGIANTS

Name	Location	Spectral Classification	Distance	Visual Magnitude	Absolute Magnitude
Alpha Camelopardalis	Camelopardalis	0.95 Ia	6,940 light-years	4.29	−6.2
Zeta Orionis	Orion	0.95 Ib	820 light-years	1.68	−5.9
Epsilon Orionis (Alnilam)	Orion	B0 Ia	1,340 light-years	1.62	−6.2
Kappa Cassiopeiae	Cassiopeia	B1 Ia	4,130 light-years	4.21	−6.6
Nu Scorpii	Scorpius	B2 Iv	440 light-years	4.00	−5.7
Eta Canis Majoris	Canis Major	B5 Ia	3,200 light-years	2.42	−7.0
Beta Orionis (Rigel)	Orion	B8 Ia	770 light-years	0.19	−7.1
Sigma Cygni	Cygnus	B9 Ia	4,530 light-years	4.27	−7.1

BRIEF LIVES

By human standards, the Sun is unimaginably powerful. But our star cannot come close in comparison with the blue supergiants, the most powerful stars in the universe. These stellar heavyweights outdo the Sun in every respect. Blue supergiants are hotter than our star, more massive, larger, and much brighter, and they live much faster lives.

Blue supergiants are stars of spectral class O or B. To astronomers, this is a code meaning that these stars have surface temperatures that range from 20,000°F (11,000°C) to more than 100,000°F (55,500°C). Such high temperatures give these stars their bright blue-white color, and no stars are hotter than those classified as class O.

In terms of mass, blue supergiants are among the heaviest stars known. Typically, they range from five to 25 solar masses, and in some extreme cases outweigh more than 100 Suns. But it is because of their luminosity that these stars really stand out.

All hot objects, including stars, radiate energy at a rate that depends on their surface area and on the fourth power of their temperature. Thus, if the temperature of an object doubles, then the output of energy increases 16 times. Blue supergiants have the highest stellar temperatures, and their diameters are at least 20 times that of the Sun. As a result, they are exceptionally luminous. Even a modest blue supergiant is brighter than 10,000 Suns, and the most brilliant would outshine several hundred thousand Sun-like stars put together.

FAST WORKERS

Such power comes at a price, though. And the blue supergiants pay for their supremacy with a lifetime only one-thousandth that of our Sun. These stars are so massive that, in order to counterbalance their tendency to collapse under their own weight, their cores have to produce an enormous amount of outward pressure.

As in all stars, that pressure is generated by nuclear reactions—in blue supergiants, the conversion of helium into carbon. But because the cores of blue supergiants are under so much more stress than in lesser stars, the nuclear reactions in blue supergiants must work faster in order to generate pressure and prevent collapse. So these blue stars consume their nuclear fuel at phenomenal rates, and use up that fuel far more quickly than a star like the Sun.

This high luminosity has other implications. Photons—particles of light and all other forms of electromagnetic radiation—can exert pressure like a hail of bullets. The higher the temperature, the greater the photon energy, and the higher the luminosity, the more photons per second a star emits. So a high temperature and luminosity combine to produce a very powerful radiation pressure.

In the case of a blue supergiant, the star's own emitted radiation as it leaves the surface can literally push atmospheric gas away and blast it into space. The result is a star that slowly evaporates. The star creates a nebulous shell of gas around it, as happens with the Wolf-Rayet stars.

Blue supergiants are exceedingly rare. In a typical region of the Milky Way, only 0.1 percent of the stars will be blue supergiants, and most will be of class B. O-type stars are even more uncommon, numbering less than one in four million stars. But the tremendous luminosity of these stars means that, despite their scarcity, they are easy to spot in the depths of space. Some blue supergiants can even be seen individually in distant galaxies.

DOWN AT HEEL

RIGEL, ONE OF THE MOST FAMOUS STARS IN THE SKY, IS A BLUE SUPERGIANT 1,400 LIGHT-YEARS AWAY IN THE CONSTELLATION ORION, THE HUNTER (RIGHT). RIGEL IS ONE OF THE TWO BRIGHTEST STARS IN ORION—THE OTHER BEING THE RED SUPERGIANT BETELGEUSE. RIGEL MARKS THE HUNTER'S HEEL. TWENTY TIMES THE MASS OF THE SUN AND 150,000 TIMES AS LUMINOUS, RIGEL IS THE SEVENTH BRIGHTEST STAR IN THE ENTIRE SKY AND IS EASILY SEEN WITH THE UNAIDED EYE.

Blue supergiants shrink and shed their outer layers over tens of thousands of years. In nebula NGC 6164-6165, the contracting central star has blasted out gas to form three shells.

STELLAR COMPARISON

Unlike cooler stars, the outermost layers of blue stars are not convective—they do not transfer heat outward in a cellular pattern. So these stars are unable to generate magnetic fields in their interiors. As a result, they lack the surface features—starspots—that are associated with stellar activity in cooler stars. Blue supergiants are featureless, blue-white globes.

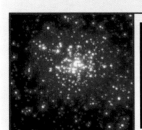

R136 IN LMC
Some 160,000 light-years away in the Large Magellanic Cloud lies a spectacular cluster of giant blue stars called R136. The cluster, embedded inside the nebula known as 30 Doradus, is a tight jumble of thousands of blue stars, some as much as 50 times heavier than the Sun.

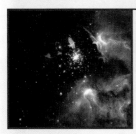

NGC 3603
This Hubble image of the galactic nebula NGC 3603 captures a blue supergiant in the process of shedding its layers into space. Called Sher 25, the star (center) is partially surrounded by a ring of gas ejected by the star as it ages.

Sun shown at same scale

blue supergiant

The Sun is 9.73 times the size of Jupiter, which in turn is 11.2 times as large as the Earth. The blue supergiant (far left), although 20 times the diameter of the Sun, is a medium-size example.

the Sun

Jupiter

Earth

PLANETARY NEBULAE

When eighteenth-century astronomers probed the skies with powerful telescopes, they found fuzzy disks unlike the pinpoints of regular stars. They called the objects planetary nebulae. But these nebulae are not planets; they are expanding clouds of gas and debris that mark the death of stars. Illuminated by the stellar remnants within them, the intricate and beautiful nebulae are short-lived, destined to soon disperse into invisibility. The material they contain, though, will be recycled in the stars—and worlds—of the next generation, eventually being sucked toward newly forming objects.

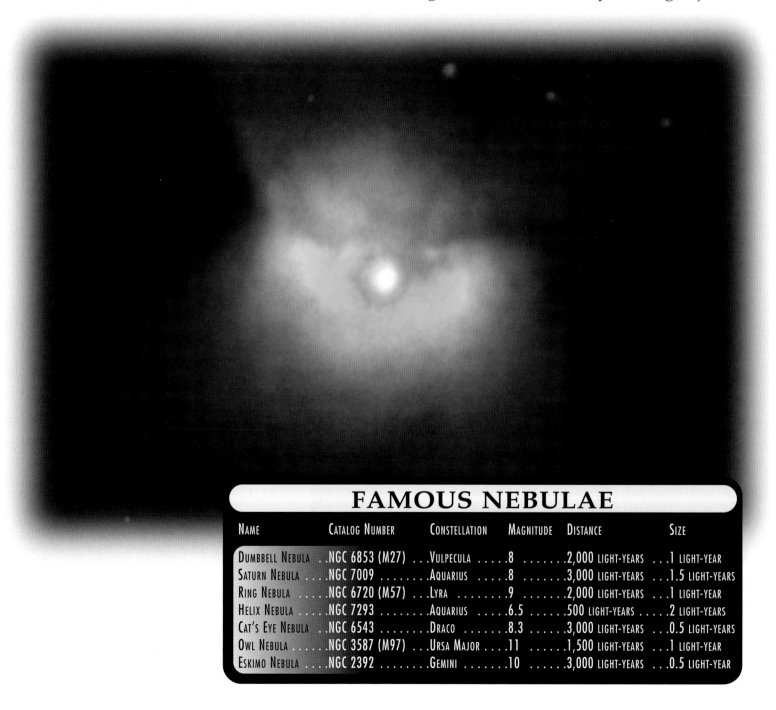

FAMOUS NEBULAE

Name	Catalog Number	Constellation	Magnitude	Distance	Size
Dumbbell Nebula	NGC 6853 (M27)	Vulpecula	.8	2,000 light-years	1 light-year
Saturn Nebula	NGC 7009	Aquarius	.8	3,000 light-years	1.5 light-years
Ring Nebula	NGC 6720 (M57)	Lyra	.9	2,000 light-years	1 light-year
Helix Nebula	NGC 7293	Aquarius	6.5	500 light-years	2 light-years
Cat's Eye Nebula	NGC 6543	Draco	8.3	3,000 light-years	0.5 light-years
Owl Nebula	NGC 3587 (M97)	Ursa Major	11	1,500 light-years	1 light-year
Eskimo Nebula	NGC 2392	Gemini	10	3,000 light-years	0.5 light-year

THE LAST SUNSET

For most of its life, a star burns with the light of nuclear fusion as hydrogen in its core is converted into helium. The energy of the reaction creates an outward pressure that prevents the star from collapsing under its own weight. But when the hydrogen runs out, the star starts to shrink. Paradoxically, the shrinkage itself generates more light and heat, and the outer layers puff out enormously. The star becomes a red giant.

If the star is very massive, it will one day destroy itself in the spectacular blast of a supernova. Moderate-sized stars—the Sun, for example—keep expanding until their outermost layers have escaped completely into space. Only the hot core remains. But it still has enough energy to flood its neighborhood with ultraviolet radiation. This energy lights up the expanding gas. Many light-years distant, astronomers on Earth detect a planetary nebula.

The term was coined in 1785 by British astronomer William Herschel, who noted the resemblance of the objects he observed to hazy planets, though he knew they were not planets. But to find out what planetary nebulae really were, astronomers had to wait for more powerful telescopes and modern astrophysical theories.

STRANGE SHAPES

Those theories certainly account for the simplest planetary nebulae. But better telescopes have brought problems as well as solutions, by revealing that not all planetary nebulae are just expanding shells.

Most planetary nebulae have some kind of symmetry. But in many cases the structure is far more complex than a simple shell. Some are hourglass-shaped. Others appear to spout distinct jets of material, and others still have intricate elliptical patterns.

Astronomers still cannot explain how all these features arise. Probably, the stars that create the nebulae do not eject their gas into space at equal speeds and densities in every direction. The one common factor they share is the extraordinary beauty of their final expanding shrouds.

The material that constitutes planetary nebulae is very thin. Their great size—they can be up to two light-years across—means that the star matter they

WHAT IF?

...WE COULD WATCH WHAT HAPPENS TO NEBULAR GAS?

A planetary nebula may mark the end of a star, but not that star's material. The universe is the ultimate recycling machine and does not like waste.

As a planetary nebula expands into space, its material gets thinner. It is only visible because of the impact of ultraviolet radiation from the star's remains. This radiation has an ionizing effect. When a photon of ultraviolet light strikes an atom, it knocks away an outer electron. Shortly afterward, the electron rejoins its parent atom in a process known as recombination. When it does so, the atom gives off a photon of visible light.

As the nebula expands, its atoms grow farther apart, and their chance of encountering an ionizing photon diminishes. About 100,000 years after the planetary nebula is born, its gas has spread so widely that the ionization and recombination cease.

The nebula is now scarcely denser than the surrounding interstellar medium—the atoms and ions between stars—and it fades out into invisibility.

But this is not the end of the nebula's story. As the nebular gas drifts through space, it will one day encounter other clouds of gas and dust. As these clouds of gas collide, gravitational eddies will form within them. Some regions will have higher densities than others, and their greater mass will give them a greater gravitational attraction.

Out between the stars, dense areas grow denser as their gravity pulls in more of the surrounding material—increasing their ability to grow denser still. After a few million years, these denser regions are substantial enough to collapse under their own gravity. At the collapsing cloud's center, a new star is born from the ashes and the cycle begins afresh.

contain is spread thinner than the best vacuums that scientists can create on Earth. Mostly, the nebulae are made up of hydrogen and helium. But they also contain heavier elements, notably oxygen and nitrogen. In the next round of star formation, these extra elements will give the next generation of stars a more complex chemical structure. And some of the material, once the discarded mantle of a dead star, may wind up as part of a planet circling a newborn sun.

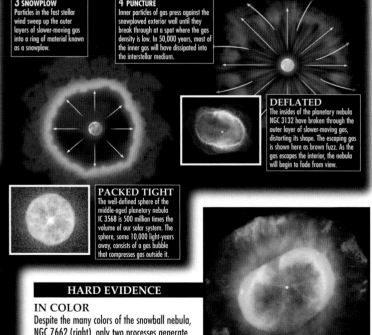

3 SNOWPLOW
Particles in the fast stellar wind sweep up the outer layers of slower-moving gas into a ring of material known as a snowplow.

4 PUNCTURE
Inner particles of gas press against the snowplowed exterior wall until they break through at a spot where the gas density is low. In 50,000 years, most of the inner gas will have dissipated into the interstellar medium.

DEFLATED
The insides of the planetary nebula NGC 3132 have broken through the outer layer of slower-moving gas, distorting its shape. The escaping gas is shown here as brown fuzz. As the gas escapes the interior, the nebula will begin to fade from view.

PACKED TIGHT
The well-defined sphere of the middle-aged planetary nebula IC 3568 is 500 million times the volume of our solar system. The sphere, some 10,000 light-years away, consists of a gas bubble that compresses gas outside it.

FINAL PUFF

1 EXPLOSION
As a red giant star dies, it ejects its outer layers into space.

Planetary nebulae are clouds of gas expelled by old stars. How these clouds intermingle determines their shape.

2 SWELLING BUBBLE
Millions of years after the first ejection, the dust clears, and the intense starlight propels a second wave of particles up to a thousand times faster than the first wave.

WELLING UP
The elliptical gas bubble in this young planetary nebula, NGC 7027, is yellow in optical light. The bubble is forced outward by the particles of radiation called photons. In sufficient quantities, a hail of photons gradually beats the bubble outward.

HARD EVIDENCE

IN COLOR
Despite the many colors of the snowball nebula, NGC 7662 (right), only two processes generate all the radiation of all planetary nebulae: ionization and recombination. Inside the nebula, a white dwarf star emits ultraviolet radiation. On contact with atoms of gas out in the nebula, this radiation knocks off some electrons, leaving behind positively-charged ions. Eventually, these ions will attract free-floating negatively-charged electrons. When ion and electron recombine, they emit visible light. It is this "recombination radiation" that illuminates the nebula. Recombining oxygen ions emit green light; recombining hydrogen ions, blue light; and recombining nitrogen ions, red light.

WHITE AND BLACK DWARFS

A star dies. It collapses under its own weight until its super-compressed matter occupies a sphere no bigger than an Earth-sized planet—a white dwarf. Their crowded interiors generate no new energy, so white dwarfs shine merely as the energy that has built up inside them slowly leaks through the packed interior and into space. But these objects will not shine forever. Gradually, over many billions of years, they will fade from view. The end product is a black dwarf—cool, dark, and invisible.

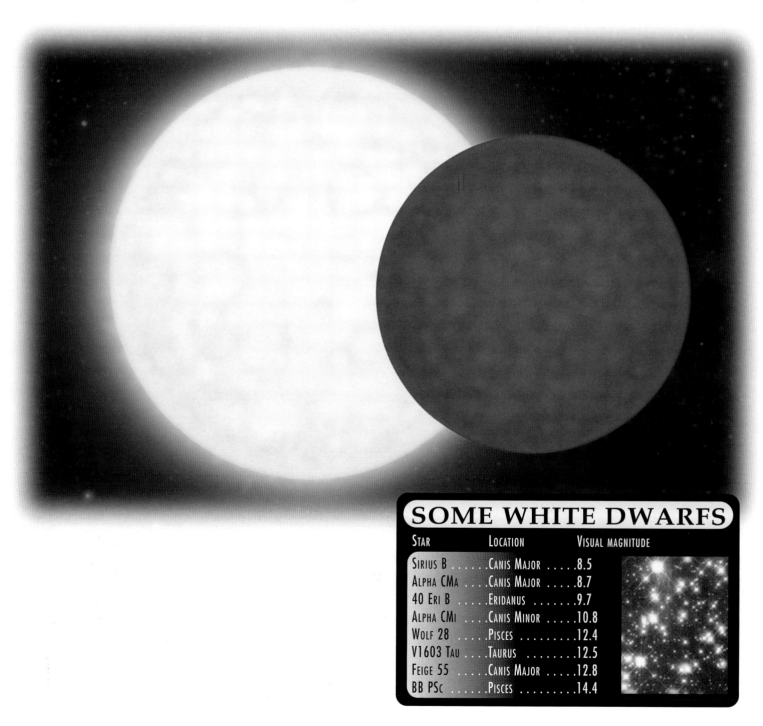

SOME WHITE DWARFS

Star	Location	Visual magnitude
Sirius B	Canis Major	8.5
Alpha CMa	Canis Major	8.7
40 Eri B	Eridanus	9.7
Alpha CMi	Canis Minor	10.8
Wolf 28	Pisces	12.4
V1603 Tau	Taurus	12.5
Feige 55	Canis Major	12.8
BB Psc	Pisces	14.4

STELLAR EVENING

Hydrogen and helium sustain the nuclear reactions of a star like our Sun, and produce the energy that holds it in shape despite the crushing force of its own gravity. But when the star has exhausted its supply of this material, it becomes a victim of its own immense mass. Gravity finally wins, and the star begins to shrink. The end result is a super-compressed sphere the size of a small planet but millions of times denser—an object called a white dwarf. A spoonful of typical white dwarf matter would tip the scales at several tons. No terrestrial object can ever become this dense. But white dwarfs are not made of terrestrial materials, or even of ordinary matter.

Normal matter is composed of atoms. Each atom has a nucleus surrounded by a cloud of negatively charged particles called electrons. In everyday objects, these electrons are so far apart that the material they make up is essentially just empty space. But inside a white dwarf, atoms are so tightly compressed that their electron clouds mingle. At these densities, a concept known as the Pauli exclusion principle comes into play.

This principle essentially states that there is a minimum distance separating two electrons. If there were no such limit, all atoms would collapse to become as simple as hydrogen, and complex chemistry would cease to exist. But when electrons are forced together, they repel each other with their own force, which is known as degeneracy pressure.

TO THE LIMIT

In a white dwarf, where gravity has compressed the star's atoms until the electrons are as close together as they can get, it is this degeneracy pressure—the resistance of the electrons to being any closer together—that prevents any further collapse of the star.

As far as their physical dimensions are concerned, white dwarfs share a strange property. A white dwarf with the same mass as the Sun would be 90 percent the size of the Earth. But a heavier white dwarf, with 1.2 solar masses, has a more powerful gravitational pull because of its extra mass. The force of gravity compresses the heavier star even more, shrinking its diameter to only about 60 percent of Earth's. In other words, the more massive white dwarfs are, the smaller they are—and the higher their internal pressure is.

Using this relationship, the Indian-American astrophysicist Subrahmanyan Chandrasekhar (1910–95) showed that there is a maximum possible mass for a white dwarf, and thus a minimum possible radius. The Chandrasekhar limit states that if the star contains more than 1.4 solar masses, its gravity becomes so overwhelming that even degeneracy pressure cannot support its weight. The star collapses further, until it becomes a neutron star, a tiny, superdense ball hundreds of times smaller than even a white dwarf.

CLASSIFYING DWARFS

NORMAL STARS ARE CLASSIFIED BY THEIR DIFFERENT COLORS (RIGHT). WHITE DWARFS USED TO BE CLASSIFIED IN A SIMILAR WAY. BUT IN 1983, US ASTRONOMER ED SION PROPOSED A NEW CLASSIFICATION THAT CONSISTED OF THREE CAPITAL LETTERS. THE FIRST LETTER, D, STANDS FOR "DEGENERATE," THE SECOND IS A CODE THAT DESCRIBES THE SPECTRUM OF THE STAR, AND THE LAST LETTER DESCRIBES WHETHER THE SMALL STAR HAS ANY PECULIAR FEATURES, SUCH AS A STRONG MAGNETIC FIELD.

HARD EVIDENCE

NEBULAE

When a star like the Sun dies, it swells into a red giant and then puffs off its tenuous gas envelope to expose its core. The core is so hot that it energizes the discarded gas that surrounds it and makes it glow brilliantly to form a bright shell—a planetary nebula, like the Dumbbell nebula (right). These objects are common in the galaxy. In many cases, the central star—that is, the core of the original dying star—is either a white dwarf, or is well on the way to becoming one.

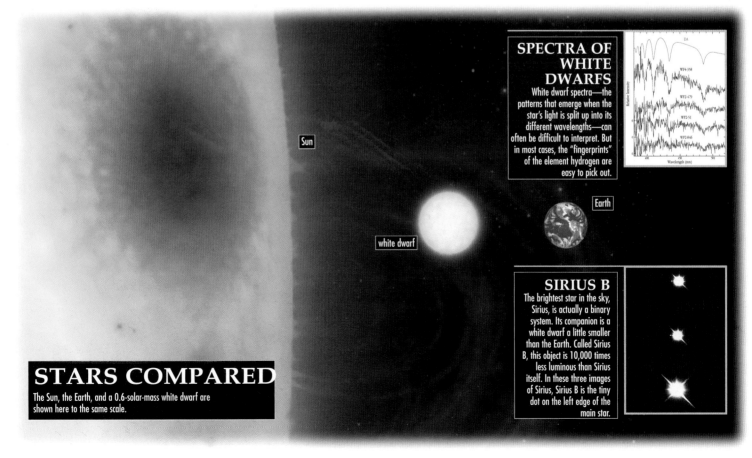

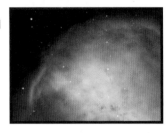

SPECTRA OF WHITE DWARFS

White dwarf spectra—the patterns that emerge when the star's light is split up into its different wavelengths—can often be difficult to interpret. But in most cases, the "fingerprints" of the element hydrogen are easy to pick out.

Sun

white dwarf

Earth

STARS COMPARED

The Sun, the Earth, and a 0.6-solar-mass white dwarf are shown here to the same scale.

SIRIUS B

The brightest star in the sky, Sirius, is actually a binary system. Its companion is a white dwarf a little smaller than the Earth. Called Sirius B, this object is 10,000 times less luminous than Sirius itself. In these three images of Sirius, Sirius B is the tiny dot on the left edge of the main star.

SUPERNOVA

ot even stars live forever—and the bigger the star, the more spectacular its demise. When a star is at least eight times the size of our Sun, it can end in a detonation so powerful that it temporarily outshines every other star in its galaxy. Called a supernova, such a blast is rare: only six supernovae have been observed in the Milky Way during all of recorded history. Over galactic timescales, though, these catastrophes have created the elemental material from which new generations of stars, planets, and even life itself have eventually been formed.

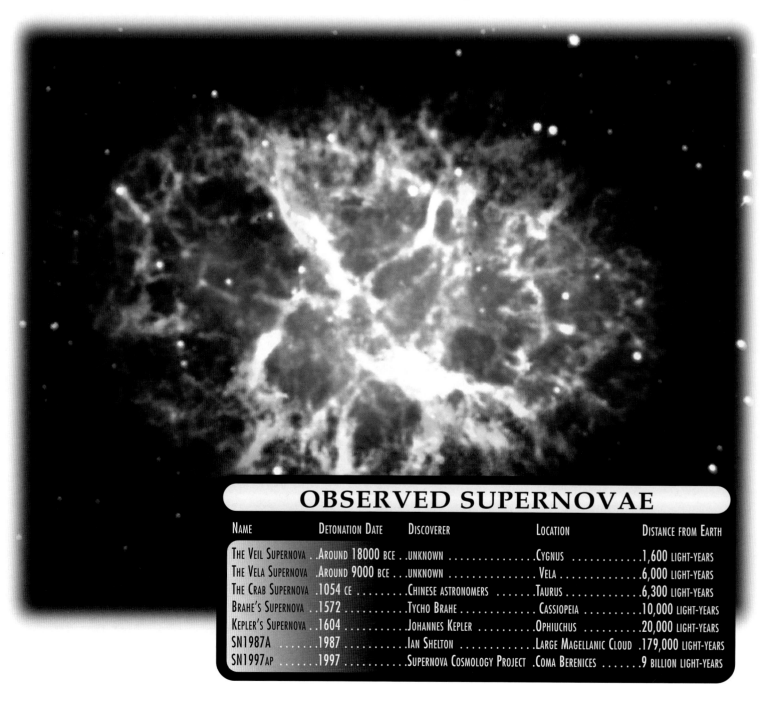

OBSERVED SUPERNOVAE

Name	Detonation Date	Discoverer	Location	Distance from Earth
The Veil Supernova	Around 18000 bce	unknown	Cygnus	1,600 light-years
The Vela Supernova	Around 9000 bce	unknown	Vela	6,000 light-years
The Crab Supernova	1054 ce	Chinese astronomers	Taurus	6,300 light-years
Brahe's Supernova	1572	Tycho Brahe	Cassiopeia	10,000 light-years
Kepler's Supernova	1604	Johannes Kepler	Ophiuchus	20,000 light-years
SN1987A	1987	Ian Shelton	Large Magellanic Cloud	179,000 light-years
SN1997ap	1997	Supernova Cosmology Project	Coma Berenices	9 billion light-years

SUPERNOVA EXPLOSION

PAST BANG

In 1054 CE, startled Chinese astronomers recorded the appearance of a new star in the constellation of Taurus. In fact, a star had died in a supernova explosion. A millennium later, the expanding cloud of debris is known as the Crab Nebula.

SUPERNOVA 1987A

In 1987, a star in the Large Magellanic Cloud blew itself to pieces. Although the explosion was 179,000 light-years away, it was the brightest "nearby" supernova in 400 years. After the blast, a spherical shell of gas and debris expanded into space, captured in this false-color image taken by the Hubble Space Telescope. In a few million years, the shell will become so diffuse that it will no longer be visible.

TOTAL DESTRUCTION
A few minutes after a star goes supernova, a planet at Jupiter's distance from the Sun is annihilated by an expanding cloud of debris, gas, and radiation. The radiation could threaten life light-years away.

HARD CORE
A surge of energy blows the outer layers of the star away from the superdense neutron core that will survive the supernova explosion. The energy, generated by the star's gravitational collapse, creates new elements and leaves behind a neutron star only a few miles across.

DEATH OF A STAR

The titanic explosion astronomers call a supernova marks the destruction of a star that has run out of fuel—and time. Stars feed on hydrogen, the most abundant element in the universe. Nuclear reactions at a star's core fuse atoms of hydrogen together to make helium. The process generates an enormous amount of heat, as well as an outward pressure of escaping radiation that prevents the star from collapsing under its own colossal weight.

Stars big enough to turn supernova—at least eight times as massive as our Sun—have relatively short lives. Their core temperatures are very high, and they burn through their hydrogen fuel supply quickly. When their

hydrogen has all fused to helium—perhaps after only 10 million years—the star has little time left. Another nuclear-fusion reaction turns the helium core into carbon, which yields enough energy to buy the star another half million years. When the helium has gone, the next reaction, carbon into neon, lasts only a few centuries. It takes only about a year to turn the neon into oxygen and around six months to burn the oxygen into silicon. The final reaction, which converts silicon to iron, runs to completion in just one day.

No further atomic reactions are possible: iron is stable, even in the furnace of a stellar core. In addition, quite abruptly, there is no internal energy available to counterbalance the force of gravity, and the star collapses

inward—within just a few seconds. As it collapses, the inner core becomes ever denser. Soon, its component atoms are squeezed so tightly together that nothing is left but the subatomic particles called neutrons, and the core can collapse no farther.

Infalling material now bounces back at speeds of up to 150 million miles (240 million km) per hour. A devastating shock wave blows the defunct star apart in an immense eruption that for a time can outshine the light from an entire galaxy. The cataclysmic energies involved in the final destructive moments are enough to break through the barrier of iron's nuclear stability—a supernova is the only place in the universe where elements heavier than iron can be made.

Only the star's core remains. This so-called neutron star may contain 20 percent of the original star's mass, squeezed into a dim cosmic tombstone only a few miles across. Meanwhile, gas, debris, and radiation from the supernova spread outward. The remnants collide with preexisting interstellar gas, generating shock waves that compact the gas and often lead to the formation of new stars. Thus star death leads to star birth—and more.

During a supernova explosion, the new elements forged in the ruined star are scattered like windborne seeds throughout space. In time, these elements will make planets like our Earth and living things like ourselves.

NEUTRON STARS

Neutron stars are the collapsed remains of giant stars that ended their days in supernova explosions. By cosmic standards a neutron star is tiny—only a few miles across—and glows so dimly that it is barely visible. Yet neutron stars have their own ways to make themselves known. Their incredible density means that just a cupful of their matter weighs more than a 2-mile (3.2 km)-wide asteroid. And although neutron stars are usually too small to be seen, their gravity has a marked effect on the orbits of nearby stars, which can make them visible through telescopes.

MATTER DENSITIES COMPARED

OBJECT	MASS OF 1 CU FT (0.02 M³)
ORION NEBULA	1/1,000,000,000,000 OZ/2.8×10^{-11} G
EARTH	343.75 LB (156 KG)
SUN'S CORE	5.125 TONS (4.65 T)
WHITE DWARF STAR	31,250 TONS (28,350 T)
NEUTRON STAR	31.25 TRILLION TONS (28.35 TRILLION T)

TINY, HEAVY, DENSE

Forged by a supernova explosion into some of the heaviest material in the universe, a neutron star crams enough matter to build three Suns into a smooth, spinning ball that may be less than 20 miles (32 km) in diameter. At such a density, the fundamental structure of matter is altered. Atoms no longer exist. Their component electrons and protons are gone, crushed by titanic pressure into neutrons that are themselves packed together almost as tightly as they would be inside a regular atomic nucleus. Tiny by the standards of its stellar neighbors, a neutron star is really a gigantic subatomic particle.

A neutron star begins life as the core of a giant star—at least 10 times as massive as the Sun. Within the giant, the gravitational pressures are enormous. So long as the star has hydrogen to burn, the outward pressure of the radiation created by nuclear fusion counterbalances the inward pressure of the star's mass. But when the star runs out of fuel, it collapses under the force of its own colossal gravity, and the matter in the core rapidly undergoes a remarkable transformation.

In regular atoms, electrons orbit a tiny, dense nucleus that is made up of protons and neutrons. Compared with the size of the nucleus, the electrons are a vast distance away: atoms consist mainly of empty space. But inside a star, the enormous heat and pressure separate out the atomic nuclei into ultra-dense particles that exist in a kind of electron soup—a state known as plasma.

Even in the thick plasma at the heart of a star, powerful subatomic forces keep the various particles apart; at a subatomic level, the plasma deep inside a star is still mostly empty space.

But in a dying giant star, the repulsive force between protons and electrons is overcome by the irresistible force of the star's gravitational collapse. Suddenly, squeezed together, they combine into neutrons with no space at all between them. The core of the dying star transforms itself into a new kind of matter of unimaginable density, and a new neutron star is born.

COSMIC CLUES

The first real clues to the existence of neutron stars came from their effect on other stars. When a neutron star orbits a normal companion star that is losing material as it ages, the neutron star's powerful gravity tears long ribbons of gas from its neighbor and draws it into orbit around itself. The enormous gravitational pull causes the gas to whirl around at very high speeds, which creates so much friction between its atoms that they emit easily detectable X-rays in all directions.

The neutron star also affects the orbit of its companion, causing it to "wobble" as seen from Earth. Astronomers can measure this wobble and deduce the mass and location of the invisible neutron star that is causing it. The Hubble Space Telescope has even succeeded in detecting a lone neutron star, betrayed by the X-rays that it gives off, simply because it is so incredibly hot—measuring a staggering 1.2 million °F (660,000°C).

NEUTRONIUM

A MICROSCOPICALLY THIN LAYER OF NEUTRON STAR MATERIAL WOULD MAKE IMPENETRABLE ARMOR PLATE. THE ONLY PROBLEM IS THE MATERIAL'S WEIGHT: A TANK PROTECTED WITH A SUPER-DENSE "NEUTRONIUM" COATING WOULD SINK TO THE CENTER OF THE EARTH.

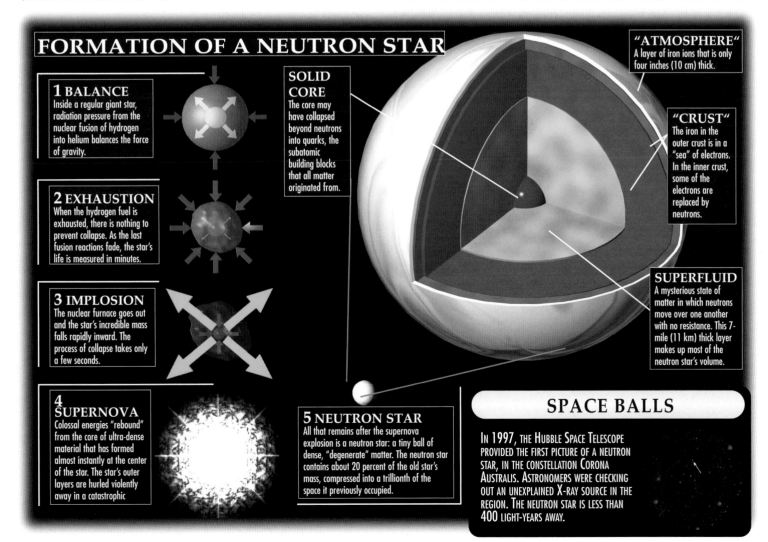

FORMATION OF A NEUTRON STAR

1 BALANCE
Inside a regular giant star, radiation pressure from the nuclear fusion of hydrogen into helium balances the force of gravity.

2 EXHAUSTION
When the hydrogen fuel is exhausted, there is nothing to prevent collapse. As the last fusion reactions fade, the star's life is measured in minutes.

3 IMPLOSION
The nuclear furnace goes out and the star's incredible mass falls rapidly inward. The process of collapse takes only a few seconds.

4 SUPERNOVA
Colossal energies "rebound" from the core of ultra-dense material that has formed almost instantly at the center of the star. The star's outer layers are hurled violently away in a catastrophic

SOLID CORE
The core may have collapsed beyond neutrons into quarks, the subatomic building blocks that all matter originated from.

5 NEUTRON STAR
All that remains after the supernova explosion is a neutron star: a tiny ball of dense, "degenerate" matter. The neutron star contains about 20 percent of the old star's mass, compressed into a trillionth of the space it previously occupied.

"ATMOSPHERE"
A layer of iron ions that is only four inches (10 cm) thick.

"CRUST"
The iron in the outer crust is in a "sea" of electrons. In the inner crust, some of the electrons are replaced by neutrons.

SUPERFLUID
A mysterious state of matter in which neutrons move over one another with no resistance. This 7-mile (11 km) thick layer makes up most of the neutron star's volume.

SPACE BALLS

IN 1997, THE HUBBLE SPACE TELESCOPE PROVIDED THE FIRST PICTURE OF A NEUTRON STAR, IN THE CONSTELLATION CORONA AUSTRALIS. ASTRONOMERS WERE CHECKING OUT AN UNEXPLAINED X-RAY SOURCE IN THE REGION. THE NEUTRON STAR IS LESS THAN 400 LIGHT-YEARS AWAY.

PULSARS

orged in the fire of a supernova explosion, a pulsar is the core of what was once a giant star. These small super-dense objects spin rapidly—typically once every second—and they are surrounded by some of the most powerful magnetic fields known to science.

As a pulsar spins, narrow beams of radio waves are emitted from its magnetic poles. If the beam is pointing in the Earth's direction, astronomers can detect the star's radio emission blinking on and off with the timekeeping precision of an atomic clock.

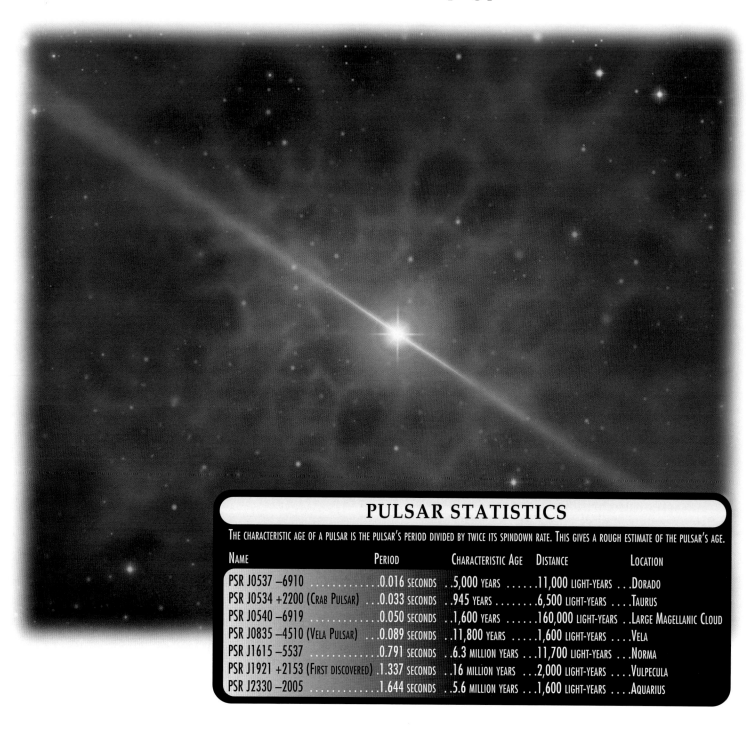

PULSAR STATISTICS

THE CHARACTERISTIC AGE OF A PULSAR IS THE PULSAR'S PERIOD DIVIDED BY TWICE ITS SPINDOWN RATE. THIS GIVES A ROUGH ESTIMATE OF THE PULSAR'S AGE.

Name	Period	Characteristic Age	Distance	Location
PSR J0537 −6910	0.016 seconds	5,000 years	11,000 light-years	Dorado
PSR J0534 +2200 (Crab Pulsar)	0.033 seconds	945 years	6,500 light-years	Taurus
PSR J0540 −6919	0.050 seconds	1,600 years	160,000 light-years	Large Magellanic Cloud
PSR J0835 −4510 (Vela Pulsar)	0.089 seconds	11,800 years	1,600 light-years	Vela
PSR J1615 −5537	0.791 seconds	6.3 million years	11,700 light-years	Norma
PSR J1921 +2153 (First discovered)	1.337 seconds	16 million years	2,000 light-years	Vulpecula
PSR J2330 −2005	1.644 seconds	5.6 million years	1,600 light-years	Aquarius

COSMIC CLOCKS

Was a radio source that flashed on and off regularly—once every 1.33730119 seconds exactly—the first sign of alien intelligence? English graduate student Jocelyn Bell of Cambridge University chanced upon the source in 1967. She and her colleagues realized that the signal they had detected was not local—it was not, say, a satellite. This regular signal had to be from space. Within a few weeks, three more such objects with comparable periods were discovered. This strange radio source was an entirely new natural phenomenon. Bell's research group named these objects pulsating radio sources, or pulsars.

At first, astronomers thought that the modulations were emanating from white dwarf stars—the highly condensed remains of the cores of dead stars—that changed their radius very rapidly with strict periodicity. But some pulsars had periods too small to be explained as pulsating white dwarfs—the stress of such a rapid oscillation would break a white dwarf apart.

Therefore, pulsars had to be even smaller and denser objects. The only objects that would fit the bill were neutron stars, extremely small super-dense objects created when a massive dying star implodes under its own gravity. But when the first pulsars were discovered in 1967, nobody had ever seen a neutron star. Although the existence of neutron stars was predicted by Swiss astronomer Fritz Zwicky (1898–1974) in the 1930s, many astronomers in the 1960s still saw these objects as conjectural.

IN A SPIN

In 1968, the Crab Nebula—a supernova remnant whose light explosion was observed on Earth in 1054—was found to contain a pulsar. This pulsar, like some others, had a period much too small to be explained by a pulsating white dwarf. It had to be a neutron star. So, if pulsars were neutron stars, the next problem was to explain the pulsations.

Pulsars do not actually pulsate. The modulations are caused by rapid rotation. Just as ice skaters spin faster by pulling in their arms, so a star's core spins more rapidly as it shrinks to a 10-mile (16 km) wide neutron star. No white dwarf could rotate this quickly without

flying apart. The shrinking also squeezes the star's original magnetic field into a much smaller space, increasing it by factors exceeding a billion. A combination of rapid rotation and a powerful magnetic field strength creates a dynamo action that generates an equally intense electric field that surrounds the neutron star. This electric field tears away charged particles—electrons—from the fabric of the neutron star. The

electrons move upward near the magnetic poles, where the magnetic field accelerates them away from the polar regions along the magnetic field lines. Magnetism forces these electrons to adhere to the polar field lines in a narrow cone.

A steady flow of radio emissions rises from the poles in parallel jets as the electrons emit radio waves in the direction of their motion. Because the magnetic axis

is tilted in relation to the spin axis, these jets sweep across space like a cosmic lighthouse—but emit radio rather than light waves. If the magnetic axis is within the line of sight from Earth, then each time a pole comes into sight, we can detect a jet. Our galaxy, the Milky Way, may contain as many as 100,000 active pulsars at any given time—but many are invisible to us because their magnetic axes are pointing away from the Earth.

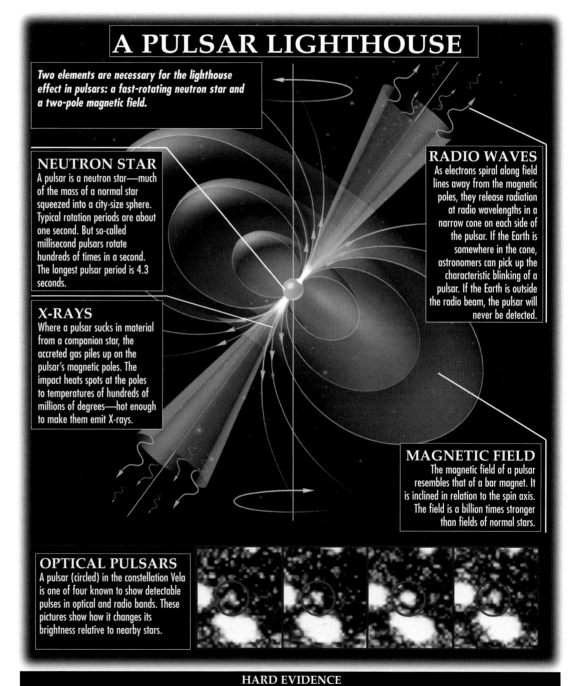

A PULSAR LIGHTHOUSE

Two elements are necessary for the lighthouse effect in pulsars: a fast-rotating neutron star and a two-pole magnetic field.

NEUTRON STAR
A pulsar is a neutron star—much of the mass of a normal star squeezed into a city-size sphere. Typical rotation periods are about one second. But so-called millisecond pulsars rotate hundreds of times in a second. The longest pulsar period is 4.3 seconds.

X-RAYS
Where a pulsar sucks in material from a companion star, the accreted gas piles up on the pulsar's magnetic poles. The impact heats spots at the poles to temperatures of hundreds of millions of degrees—hot enough to make them emit X-rays.

RADIO WAVES
As electrons spiral along field lines away from the magnetic poles, they release radiation at radio wavelengths in a narrow cone on each side of the pulsar. If the Earth is somewhere in the cone, astronomers can pick up the characteristic blinking of a pulsar. If the Earth is outside the radio beam, the pulsar will never be detected.

MAGNETIC FIELD
The magnetic field of a pulsar resembles that of a bar magnet. It is inclined in relation to the spin axis. The field is a billion times stronger than fields of normal stars.

OPTICAL PULSARS
A pulsar (circled) in the constellation Vela is one of four known to show detectable pulses in optical and radio bands. These pictures show how it changes its brightness relative to nearby stars.

HARD EVIDENCE

LITTLE GREEN MEN

Jocelyn Bell (right) stumbled upon the first pulsar during a radio sky survey in 1967. She and her colleagues in the Hewish group were mapping the sky at radio wavelengths to observe quasars. They initially thought that the regular radio source they had detected might have been a signal from an alien intelligence. The group lightheartedly suggested that the source should be named LGM-1, in which the letters LGM stood for Little Green Men. The object is now known as CP1919.

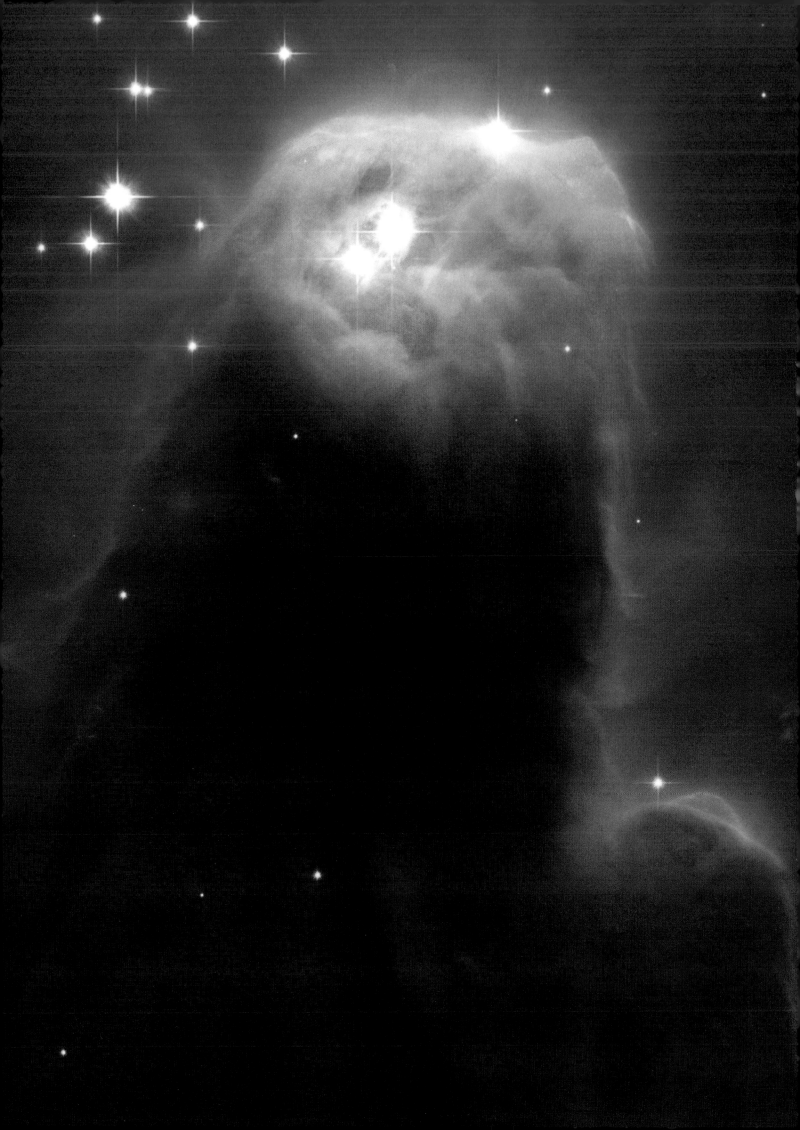

OUR GALAXY

The Milky Way we see in the sky is merely a side-on impression of the great star system in which we belong. The Milky Way galaxy is an enormous cosmic spiral containing some two hundred billion stars, and vast amounts of gas, dust, and other matter. Within the Milky Way, young stars are found in brilliant clusters, while around it orbit vast globular balls of older stars. The gas and dust form nebulae—great clouds of matter within which stars are born, and which may be illuminated spectacularly by the fierce radiation of the young stars within them. The entire system is maintained by the slow turning of the Milky Way itself, triggering episodes of collapse that turn its spiral arms into regions of continuous starbirth. At the center of the system lies an enormous hub of old red and yellow stars, concealing a violent region that contains a dormant, supermassive black hole, with the mass of several million stars lying at its heart.

This bizarre formation is actually an innocuous pillar of gas and dust. Called the Cone Nebula (NGC 2264)—so named because it has a conical shape in ground-based images—this giant pillar resides in a star-forming region of our galaxy.

STAR CLUSTERS

As well as being a beautiful sight to behold of contrasting colors and sizes, open star clusters give astronomers the chance to study a single family of stars simultaneously and to compare the differences between them. What has become apparent is that star clusters, just like human families, go through many ups and downs during the course of their existence. Some individuals are brilliant but spendthrift, while others are more sensible with their resources. And, in time, members of even the closest family unit can drift apart.

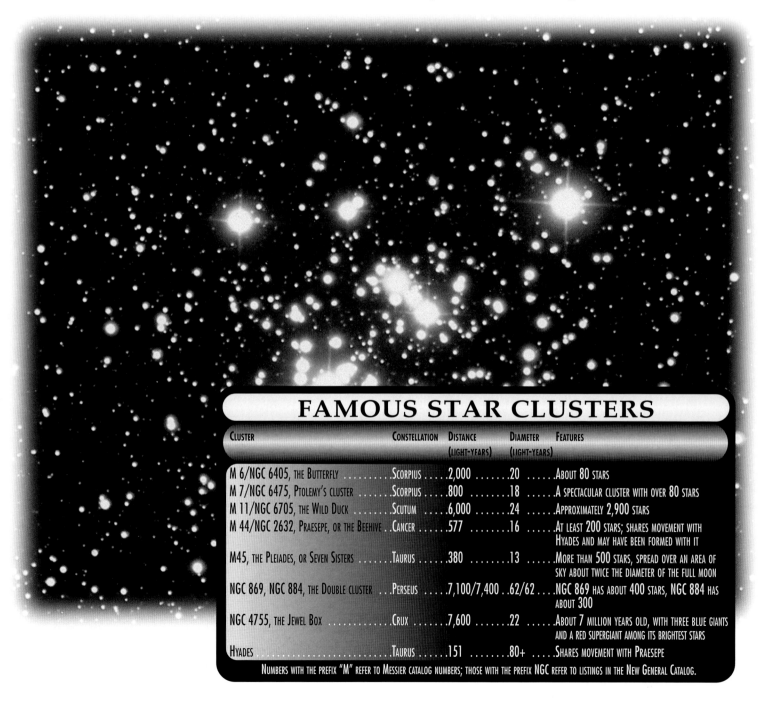

FAMOUS STAR CLUSTERS

Cluster	Constellation	Distance (light-years)	Diameter (light-years)	Features
M 6/NGC 6405, the Butterfly	Scorpius	2,000	20	About 80 stars
M 7/NGC 6475, Ptolemy's cluster	Scorpius	800	18	A spectacular cluster with over 80 stars
M 11/NGC 6705, the Wild Duck	Scutum	6,000	24	Approximately 2,900 stars
M 44/NGC 2632, Praesepe, or the Beehive	Cancer	577	16	At least 200 stars; shares movement with Hyades and may have been formed with it
M45, the Pleiades, or Seven Sisters	Taurus	380	13	More than 500 stars, spread over an area of sky about twice the diameter of the full moon
NGC 869, NGC 884, the Double cluster	Perseus	7,100/7,400	62/62	NGC 869 has about 400 stars, NGC 884 has about 300
NGC 4755, the Jewel Box	Crux	7,600	22	About 7 million years old, with three blue giants and a red supergiant among its brightest stars
Hyades	Taurus	151	80+	Shares movement with Praesepe

Numbers with the prefix "M" refer to Messier catalog numbers; those with the prefix NGC refer to listings in the New General Catalog.

BRIGHT YOUNG THINGS

Star clusters are among the most beautiful sights to be seen through a telescope and often contain dozens of brilliant stars in contrasting colors. One of the most famous lies in the constellation of the Southern Cross, where a bright red supergiant star set among blue and white neighbors has earned it the name of the Jewel Box.

Loose groups such as this are called open clusters. They can have hundreds of members and are to be found in the main disk of our galaxy. It is no accident that the stars in such clusters are so close, since they were all were born together at roughly the same time from a single cloud of gas. In their youth, the stars formed a tightly knit group, perhaps only a light-year apart, and shared the same motion through space as they orbit the galaxy.

Yet there are forces at work to separate the sibling stars, including the gravitational pull of other stars and clusters and mutual encounters between members of the same cluster. Over millions of years, these forces conspire to cause even the largest clusters to disperse. As clusters age, the stars within them also undergo a transformation. The most massive stars squander their fuel so rapidly that they cool into red supergiants within only a few million years—a phenomenon that explains the beautiful color variations within clusters such as the Jewel Box.

The importance of star clusters to astronomers lies in their common origin. Each cluster is a snapshot of stars that were born together but have developed at different rates according to their masses. In fact, much of what we know today about the evolution of stars comes from the patient study of open clusters.

HOW STAR CLUSTERS SHOW THEIR AGE

30 Doradus, part of the Tarantula Nebula in the Large Magellanic Cloud, is among the most recently formed clusters.

YOUNG CLUSTER

THE BRILLIANCE OF YOUTH...

A young star cluster, perhaps only a few million years old, is dominated by massive, brilliant blue stars that use up their fuel very quickly. The more sedate yellow and red dwarf stars will long outlive their flashy neighbors.

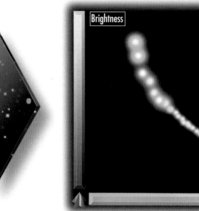

...BIG, BRIGHT, AND BLUE

When the stars in a young cluster are plotted in order of brightness, they show a smooth transition from bright, hot, and blue to dim, cool, and red. In reality the cluster may also contain many smaller red stars that are just too faint to be seen from Earth.

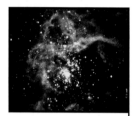

The most massive of the brilliant, blue stars in the young cluster NGC 3293 has already evolved into a red supergiant.

All the bright young stars in NGC 2818 have long since exploded. This glowing planetary nebula is the remnant of such an event.

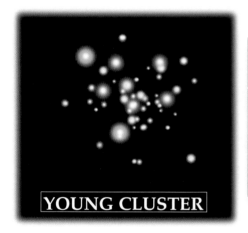

OLDER CLUSTER

OLD AGE TAKES ITS TOLL...

As a cluster ages, its most massive blue stars cool to become red supergiants and eventually explode as supernovae. The stars in the cluster may also drift apart, causing the cluster to become fainter and less clearly defined.

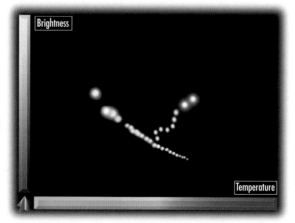

...AND THE RED STARS SHINE OUT

The brightest, hottest blue stars have gone, to be replaced by red giants of similar brightness but lower temperature. Some medium-mass stars have also begun to age, their increased brightness and redness resulting in a trail of stars toward the red-giant region.

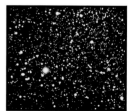

Trumpler 5 is a very old cluster, consisting only of middle-aged and low-mass stars that have drifted apart from each other.

GLOBULAR CLUSTERS

Unlike the groups of stars that make up most of the galaxies in the universe, globular clusters do not reside in the core or the arms of a galaxy. Instead, these balls of millions of stars swing around the center of the galaxy in eccentric orbits that can extend to 40,000 light-years. Because their orbits are inclined at random, the clusters appear in a spherical halo around the center of the galaxy. The most prominent globular clusters, and the easiest to study, are the ones that orbit the Milky Way.

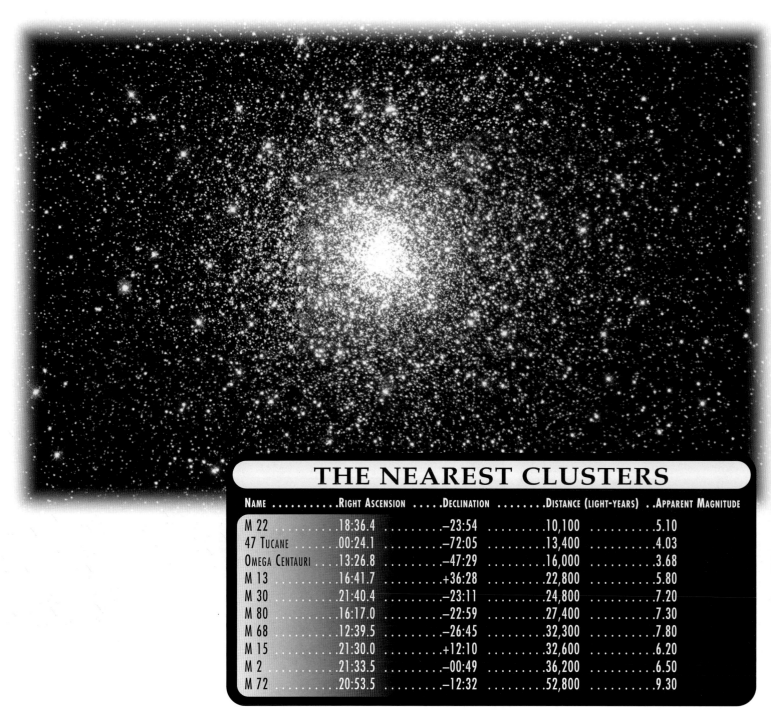

THE NEAREST CLUSTERS

Name	Right Ascension	Declination	Distance (light-years)	Apparent Magnitude
M 22	18:36.4	−23:54	10,100	5.10
47 Tucane	00:24.1	−72:05	13,400	4.03
Omega Centauri	13:26.8	−47:29	16,000	3.68
M 13	16:41.7	+36:28	22,800	5.80
M 30	21:40.4	−23:11	24,800	7.20
M 80	16:17.0	−22:59	27,400	7.30
M 68	12:39.5	−26:45	32,300	7.80
M 15	21:30.0	+12:10	32,600	6.20
M 2	21:33.5	−00:49	36,200	6.50
M 72	20:53.5	−12:32	52,800	9.30

ERRANT STARS

Spherical groups of stray stars called globular clusters are found outside the most massive parts of a galaxy, known as the halo, a spherical region around a spiral galaxy. But they are not very different from the galaxy's most central stars. Both groups formed as the galaxy was coalescing. As an enormous gas cloud slowly contracted to become the galaxy, small parts of gas on the outskirts fragmented and collapsed on their own. The larger clouds of gas collapsed into globular clusters.

A typical spiral galaxy, such as the Milky Way, will today be surrounded by a few hundred globular clusters. A giant elliptical galaxy may have 10 times as many—the total of all the galactic collisions and mergers that probably form such huge galaxies.

A single globular cluster contains between 10,000 and several million stars. Usually these star-spheres are no more than a few hundred light-years in diameter, but sometimes they measure just a few dozen light-years. Globular clusters almost always contain very old stars, formed at the same time during the initial collapse of the gas cloud. These stars are known as Population II stars and were among the first to form after the Big Bang.

We know that the stars are very old because they contain few chemical elements heavier than helium. Heavy elements such as carbon and nitrogen are made in the hearts of stars and scattered into space as the stars die. New stars—called Population I stars— form from the remains of these recycled materials.

SWEPT CLEAN

Globular clusters never get to foster new stars from the gas of old ones. The clusters are regularly swept clean as they pass through the disks of spiral galaxies. The gravity of densely packed stars in the disk pulls free gas out of a cluster—in extreme cases, the disk can tear apart the whole cluster, scattering its stars in space. According to one estimate, half of the Milky Way's 160 clusters will be destroyed this way over the next 10 billion years.

Still, not every cluster is old. We have discovered globular clusters containing young stars in the nearby Large Magellanic Cloud. One of the galaxy's star-forming clouds, the Tarantula nebula, may be a cluster in the process of forming. And a similar cloud—NGC 604— has been found in the spiral galaxy M 33.

WHAT IF?

...CLUSTER STARS TOLD THE UNIVERSE'S AGE?

Globular cluster stars can be dated by comparing their color and brightness with other stars, giving values of 14–16 billion years. A more complicated method uses the universe's expansion rate to work out the time of the Big Bang, yielding an age of 10–20 billion years.

As better estimates were made of the universe's extent, its age crept toward 10 billion years. This left an impossible scenario: globular cluster stars were older than their universe.

In the 1990s scientists uncovered evidence that the expansion of the universe has not been constant since the Big Bang, but has in fact accelerated, meaning all the old calculations of the age of the universe have been underestimates.

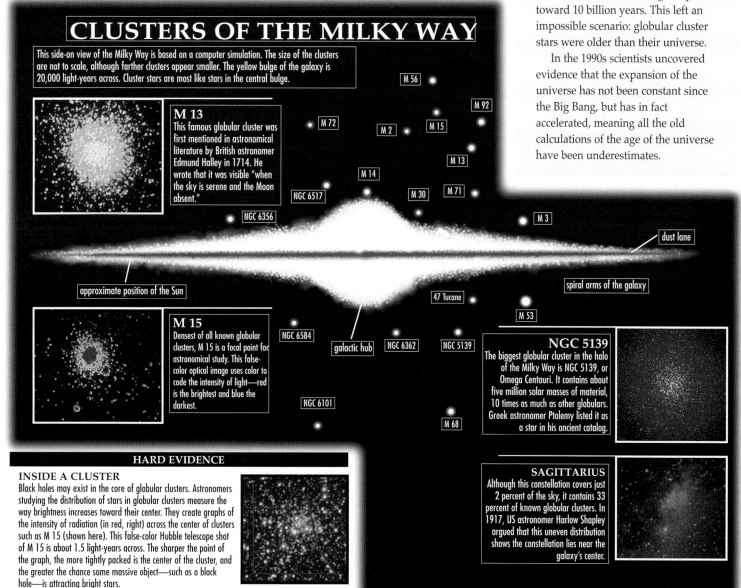

CLUSTERS OF THE MILKY WAY

This side-on view of the Milky Way is based on a computer simulation. The size of the clusters are not to scale, although farther clusters appear smaller. The yellow bulge of the galaxy is 20,000 light-years across. Cluster stars are most like stars in the central bulge.

M 13
This famous globular cluster was first mentioned in astronomical literature by British astronomer Edmund Halley in 1714. He wrote that it was visible "when the sky is serene and the Moon absent."

M 56
M 92
M 72
M 2
M 15
M 14
NGC 6517
M 30
M 71
M 13
NGC 6356
M 3

dust lane

approximate position of the Sun

spiral arms of the galaxy

M 15
Densest of all known globular clusters, M 15 is a focal point for astronomical study. This false-color optical image uses color to code the intensity of light—red is the brightest and blue the darkest.

NGC 6584
galactic hub
NGC 6362
NGC 5139
M 53
47 Tucane

NGC 6101

M 68

NGC 5139
The biggest globular cluster in the halo of the Milky Way is NGC 5139, or Omega Centauri. It contains about five million solar masses of material, 10 times as much as other globulars. Greek astronomer Ptolemy listed it as a star in his ancient catalog.

HARD EVIDENCE

INSIDE A CLUSTER
Black holes may exist in the core of globular clusters. Astronomers studying the distribution of stars in globular clusters measure the way brightness increases toward their center. They create graphs of the intensity of radiation (in red, right) across the center of clusters such as M 15 (shown here). This false-color Hubble telescope shot of M 15 is about 1.5 light-years across. The sharper the point of the graph, the more tightly packed is the center of the cluster, and the greater the chance some massive object—such as a black hole—is attracting bright stars.

SAGITTARIUS
Although this constellation covers just 2 percent of the sky, it contains 33 percent of known globular clusters. In 1917, US astronomer Harlow Shapley argued that this uneven distribution shows the constellation lies near the galaxy's center.

INTERSTELLAR MATTER

The space between the stars is not empty. Aside from dark matter, whose nature is still unknown, the unimaginably large voids that make up most of the galaxy contain a strange mixture of stray atoms, molecules, and microscopic dust particles known as the interstellar medium (ISM). The ISM is the ultimate in cosmic recycling. Although, by human standards, it is incredibly thinly scattered, this jumble of matter represents the ashes of dead stars—and the raw material for new ones.

NEBULAE COMPOSITION

Composition of Interstellar Gas (percentage of number of atoms)	
Hydrogen	92
Helium	8
Other	<1

This shows that although hydrogen accounts for most interstellar gas (and probably most interstellar matter in general), interstellar dust contains heavier elements that are probably the debris from earlier generations of stars.

Composition of Interstellar Dust (percentage of number of atoms)	
Oxygen	52
Carbon	28
Nitrogen	8
Iron	4
Silicon	3
Magnesium	3
Sulfur	2
Other	<1

BETWEEN THE STARS

Despite its apparent emptiness, interstellar space is a rich resource. Hidden within the void between stars are vast quantities of matter that are more thinly spread than any vacuum on Earth—on average, less than 20 atoms per cubic inch (1.25 per cubic centimeter). But a lot of near-nothing adds up. This seemingly unimportant material makes up as much as 10 percent of the visible mass of the entire Milky Way—enough to make 20 billion Suns.

The ISM is everywhere. In our own galaxy, it forms a 700-light-year thick disk stretching the width of the Milky Way. But the distribution within the disk is far from even. Matter clumps together in clouds called nebulae that can measure up to thousands of light-years across. At one extreme, the density of the ISM is estimated to reach 800 atoms per cubic inch (1.25 per cubic centimeter) with an average temperature as low as –300°F (–180°C). In other places, density falls, but the temperature rockets to a staggering 2 million°F (1.1 million°C).

GLOWING IN THE DARK

Much of the ISM, such as in the Orion Nebula, glows due to the stars within it. Other parts merely reflect the light of stars to one side. There are still other regions, like the dark, brooding Horsehead Nebula, that block out the light of background stars completely. From studying these different regions, astronomers now have a good idea of what the ISM consists of.

Virtually all of the gas in the ISM is hydrogen, which glows a distinctive red when it is superheated by nearby stars. Since hydrogen is the basic element from which heavier elements are created inside stars, it seems likely that most of this interstellar gas is virgin material that has yet to experience the star-formation process. But there are heavier elements, too, signifying that at least some of the gas originated in earlier generations of stars. Oxygen, for example, glows a distinctive green and is seen in the shattered remains of stars that have blown apart. Elsewhere are clouds composed only of molecules, such as the hydrogen-oxygen-carbon compound alcohol.

The ISM is not all gas. There is dust, too, composed of microscopic grains of rock and ice. Though this dust accounts for only 1 percent of the ISM's mass, it is far better at blocking out light—especially red light, which causes stars to appear redder, and thus farther away, than they really are. In fact, it is partly thanks to these and other effects of the ISM that we know as much as we do about the structure of the universe today.

INTERSTELLAR LIGHT SHOW

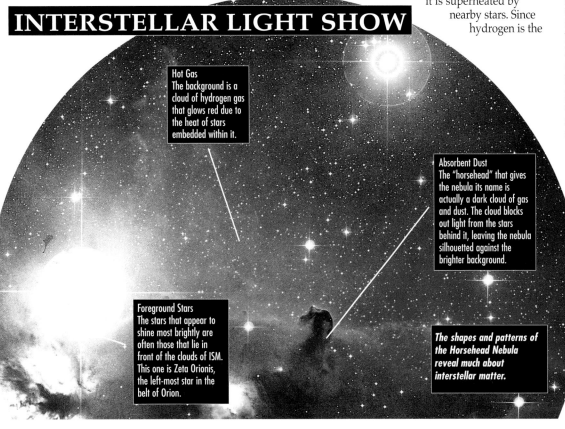

Hot Gas
The background is a cloud of hydrogen gas that glows red due to the heat of stars embedded within it.

Absorbent Dust
The "horsehead" that gives the nebula its name is actually a dark cloud of gas and dust. The cloud blocks out light from the stars behind it, leaving the nebula silhouetted against the brighter background.

Foreground Stars
The stars that appear to shine most brightly are often those that lie in front of the clouds of ISM. This one is Zeta Orionis, the left-most star in the belt of Orion.

The shapes and patterns of the Horsehead Nebula reveal much about interstellar matter.

THICK AND THIN

THE CLOUDS NEAR THE STAR RHO OPHIUCHI, 700 LIGHT-YEARS AWAY, SHOW HOW PATCHY INTERSTELLAR MATTER CAN BE. IN ONE AREA, THEY ARE THIN ENOUGH TO REVEAL THE GLOBULAR CLUSTER M4, WHICH IS 5,000 LIGHT-YEARS FARTHER AWAY. BUT NEARBY LIES A STAR WHOSE LIGHT IS WEAKENED BY THE CLOUDS BY A FACTOR OF 10,000 TRILLION (10^{16})!

HOT GAS

Hydrogen is easily the most common component of the ISM. Much of it exists in the form of giant clouds that glow red as they absorb ultraviolet energy from neighboring stars. Often, these clouds lead to the formation of new stars.

ICE PARTICLES

Astronomers think that much of the interstellar dust that is so effective at absorbing starlight consists of nothing more exotic than tar-smeared ice particles surrounding minute specks of carbon, silicon, or iron.

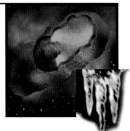

MOLECULES

Giant molecular clouds exist throughout interstellar space. Many are composed of single elements such as hydrogen, oxygen, and carbon, but in places, these elements have combined into more complex molecules, such as alcohol.

DUST AND DIRT

The Pleiades star cluster (right) contains wisp-like nebulae that were once thought to be the remains of newly formed stars. Now, astronomers think that they are simply clouds of interstellar dust into which the cluster's stars have drifted.

MILKY WAY

With both its name and appearance hinting at obscurity, the Milky Way has long been a source of fascination. Shrouded by interstellar dust clouds, what can be seen of the galaxy from Earth almost resembles a hazy glowing disc when viewed by the naked eye. While advances in telescopic technology have meant we know more about how the galaxy developed, many questions can still only be answered generally. For centuries, it was thought that the Milky Way was not very large and that our Sun was close to its center. It was not until the twentieth century that astronomers learned that the Sun was approximately 30,000 light-years from its center, and that the Milky Way spanned across an estimated diameter of 100,000 light-years.

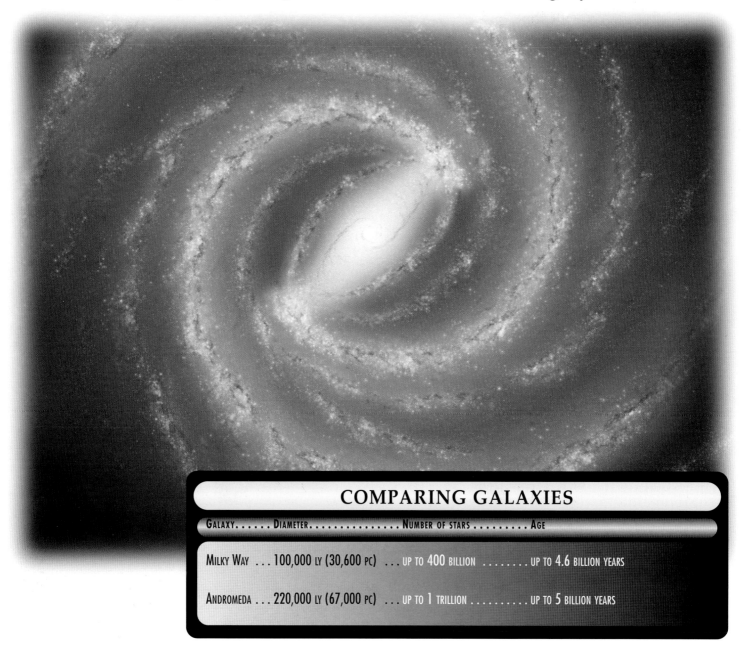

COMPARING GALAXIES

Galaxy	Diameter	Number of stars	Age
Milky Way	100,000 ly (30,600 pc)	up to 400 billion	up to 4.6 billion years
Andromeda	220,000 ly (67,000 pc)	up to 1 trillion	up to 5 billion years

EXPANDING HORIZONS

It was once thought that the Milky Way was the limit of the entire universe. For a long time, its immensity—the galaxy contains around 200 billion stars, but this figure could stretch to 400 billion in total—meant that it was hard for humans to comprehend anything bigger. Since the early twentieth century, we have known that the Milky Way is only one of many galaxies. In fact, it makes up a small section of what is known as the Local Group of over twenty galaxies—or fifty if you include dwarf galaxies, which only have a

This classification was first propositioned in the 1990s, but not confirmed until 2005, when the Spitzer Space Telescope used infrared technology to pick out the radiation, which showed this bar to be more substantial than previously believed.

Made up of over 90 percent dark matter, the visible part of the Milky Way makes up only around 10 percent of our galaxy. It is only with the aid of powerful infrared telescopes such as the Spitzer telescope that we were able to discover more about the structure of the Milky Way. Launched in 2003, it is in Earth's orbit in an Earth-trailing position. This means

Spitzer could avoid the extreme heat exposure of other telescopes and remain working for longer with lower amounts of coolant and costs. Since its launch, Spitzer's initial 2.5 year mission life has been extended indefinitely, with the telescope still sending back incredible information and images about the Milky Way and beyond.

NAMING THE MILKY WAY

Named for the Latin *via lactea*, meaning "road of milk," which was in turn taken from the Greek *galaxias kyklos* or "milky circle," the Milky Way's name resembles its hazy appearance, viewed as it is through a mist of dust, gas, and debris. The milky appearance led to its name, thought to be based on a story about the goddess Hera. When Zeus fathered Heracles by a mortal female, he put his son on the sleeping Hera's breast to suckle him. On awaking, Hera realized what Zeus had done and tore the baby from her breast. Her milk shot through the night sky, becoming the Milky Way. Many celestial bodies have mythological names, but the sheer amount means that they are now often classified by letters and numbers.

SPITZER TELESCOPE
Spitzer has told us much about the Milky Way, but has also photographed infrared images of the Andromeda and Messier 81 galaxies, as well as planetary nebula, extrasolar planets, and protostars.

BARRED SPIRALS

Stars form in a collapsing gas cloud.

If the gas cloud rotates slowly, stars quickly fall to the center.

If the gas cloud rotates quickly, stars move more slowly.

OBSERVING THE MILKY WAY
While astronomers are unable to view the entire Milky Way from Earth, what can be seen appears as a beautiful milky band that has long inspired viewers.

The rapid infall of the central stars results in a spiral galaxy.

The slow, ordered inflow of stars means they pile up into a bar.

Spiral outcome

Barred outcome

few billion stars. The Local Group also contains the Andromeda galaxy, which with the Milky Way is one of the two largest galaxies in the group. Both are significantly bigger than the 30,000 light-year diameter of an average galaxy. To give an idea of the immense size of the Local Group, it would take 2.5 million light-years to travel from the Milky Way to Andromeda. In turn, the Local Group is part of the Virgo Supercluster, which contains an estimated one hundred galaxy clusters. There are thought to be millions of these superclusters in the universe, and potentially 100 billion galaxies.

The Milky Way falls into the classification of a spiral galaxy, but it has an interesting distinction. The center is not spherical, but elongated, making it a barred spiral galaxy. Its central bar-shaped structure is the most common spiral galaxy shape. However, the bar may change over billions of years into a more regular spiral pattern.

CENTER OF THE GALAXY

Although it is on our cosmic doorstep, just twenty-six thousand to twenty-eight thousand light-years away, the center of our own galaxy remains a mystery to us. Our view of the Milky Way's core is completely hidden by bright star clouds and dark dust lanes that lie in the constellation of Sagittarius, along our line of sight toward the galactic center. But in the past few years, astronomers have finally begun to discover what lies at the heart of the Milky Way, by studying it in wavelengths of light that pass straight through the dust.

GALAXY'S HEART: SGR A

DISCOVERED	.1974
DISTANCE	.26,000–28,000 LIGHT-YEARS
DIMENSIONS	.80 AU BY 150 AU (1 AU = 93M MILES/150M KM)
ESTIMATED MASS	.2.6 MILLION SOLAR MASSES
BLACK HOLE ESTIMATED DIAMETER	.9 MILLION MILES (14.5 MILLION KM)

HIDDEN HEART

The center of the Milky Way is a strange place, full of features that astronomers do not yet fully understand. Stars become much more tightly packed close to the core. Collapsing gas clouds form giant open clusters of young stars, and there are even a few ball-shaped globular clusters, containing hundreds of thousands, or even millions, of very old red stars. The closer stars get to the center, the faster they move along their orbits.

Above and below the galactic center lie towering pillars of gas called filaments, which can be anything from a few light-years to a few hundred light-years long. These filaments follow the lines of the galaxy's magnetic field, which emerges in long, curving lines above and below its center. As the charged particles within them spiral out along the field, traveling at close to the speed of light, they emit what is called synchrotron radiation at radio wavelengths.

Some 350 light-years out from the center lies a violent object known as the Great Annihilator. Two huge jets, several light-years long, burst out from above and below a massive black hole, around 100 times the mass of the Sun, that is swallowing up surrounding gas and stars. The jets are made of antimatter created around the black hole. Where they collide with normal matter, these jets are completely destroyed, releasing high-energy gamma rays with an energy 250,000 times that of visible light—the telltale sign that antimatter is present.

INTO THE CORE

The edge of the galactic center is itself marked by a ring of gas clouds of roughly 10 light-years. These gas clouds, made mostly of hydrogen molecules and helium atoms, but with some heavier and more complex molecules including ammonia (NH3) and cyanide (CN), glow at radio wavelengths as their inner edges are heated by hot, bright stars inside them.

Within this ring of molecular clouds is a central cavity that can only be seen at infrared wavelengths. This radiation reveals that the center of the galaxy is very hot, and shows streamers of gas swirling around inside at very high speeds. This gas is being heated by some very bright, hot, mysterious objects in a cluster called IRS 16. These objects seem too bright and hot to be normal stars—they may be cannibals that have grown throughout their lives by swallowing up other stars or gas.

Close to IRS 16, at the very center of the galaxy, is an even greater mystery—a strong radio source called Sagittarius A-star, abbreviated Sgr A*. Surprisingly, Sgr A* is invisible at infrared and other wavelengths. But from the movement of stars around the galactic center, astronomers know that something at the very center of the galaxy has a mass which measures millions of times greater than the Sun, compressed into a very small point. This object is almost certainly a giant black hole, and the radio glow of Sgr A* is probably caused as material falling into the black hole is heated up and ripped apart. Why Sgr A* is such a weak source of radiation, while much smaller black holes blast out fierce X-rays, has puzzled astronomers. The black hole is probably dormant because no material has drifted into its sphere of influence recently. In the future it could flare up, allowing us to see a new X-ray source pinpointing the heart of our galaxy.

SECRETS OF THE CENTER

STAR CLUSTERS
Giant clusters of young stars form near the galactic center because of the huge amounts of gas available. Clusters like the Quintuplet (far left) and the Arches (left) will be ripped apart by gravitational forces, but are currently the brightest clusters in the galaxy.

MINI SPIRAL
Inside the galaxy's 10-light-year-wide central cavity, the stellar winds of particles gusting from the brilliant stars of the IRS 16 cluster are blowing clouds of molecular hydrogen into three ragged spiral arms.

molecular ring of gas

globular clusters

molecular ring of gas

Sgr A* within cluster IRS 16

outer lobe emitting radio waves

Although the antimatter fountain projecting from the galaxy's center is not visible to the naked eye, the rays it emits were imaged by the Compton Gamma Ray Observatory.

FILAMENTS
The Snake is a filament of ionized gas streaming out from the galactic center along a line in the galaxy's magnetic field. Unlike most filaments, however, it is not perpendicular to the galactic plane. It may run along a tangled region of magnetic field.

The central few hundred light-years of the galaxy, as revealed from Earth.

GALACTIC CENTER
At the very center of the galaxy lies IRS 16, a cluster of giant stars. Along them lies Sgr A*, a mysterious object visible at radio wavelengths only. Sgr A* is currently dormant.

HOLE TRUTH

THE PRESENCE OF A SUPERMASSIVE BLACK HOLE AT THE GALAXY'S CENTER WAS PROVEN BEYOND DOUBT IN 1998 BY US ASTRONOMER ANDREA GHEZ. BY MEASURING THE MOTIONS OF 200 STARS CLOSE TO THE CENTER OF THE MILKY WAY, GHEZ WAS ABLE TO FIND AT LEAST 20 STARS WHOSE ORBITS WERE BEING AFFECTED BY A MASSIVE OBJECT. SHE CALCULATED THAT THE OBJECT HAS A MASS 2.6 MILLION TIMES GREATER THAN THE SUN, CRAMMED INTO A SPACE JUST ONE-THIRTIETH OF A LIGHT-YEAR ACROSS. WITH SUCH AN INCREDIBLE DENSITY, IT CAN ONLY BE A BLACK HOLE.

CLASSIFYING GALAXIES

For most of history, those galaxies that were visible from Earth were nothing but faint fuzzy smears in the sky. As telescopes improved during the last century, astronomers began to be able to see detail in the smears. In 1925, American astronomer Edwin Hubble proposed a system of classifying galaxies according to their shape. Although modern astronomers have revised some of his early conclusions, today's most widely-accepted modern-day system of classification still relies on Hubble's framework.

HOW GALAXIES STACK UP

	SPIRALS	ELLIPTICALS	IRREGULARS
MASS (SOLAR MASSES)	10^9-10^{12}	10^6-10^{13}	10^8-10^{11}
LUMINOSITY (SOLAR LUMINOSITIES)	10^8-10^{11}	10^6-10^{11}	10^8-10^{11}
DIAMETER (IN 1,000S OF LIGHT-YEARS)	10–100	2–400	2–30
TYPE OF STARS (POP. I: HOT, YOUNG)	POP. II (IN HALO AND BULGE)	POP. II	MAINLY POP. I
(POP. II: OLD, FEW HEAVY ELEMENTS)	POP. I (IN DISK)		
GAS AND DUST	IN THE DISK	VERY LITTLE	THROUGHOUT
LOCATION	PRIMARILY IN REGIONS OF LOW GALACTIC DENSITY	DWARFS ARE OMNIPRESENT; LARGE ELLIPTICALS ARE USUALLY IN DENSE CLUSTERS	PRIMARILY IN REGIONS OF LOW GALACTIC DENSITY

TAKING SHAPE

The powerful telescopes that came into service on Mount Wilson, California, in the early decades of the twentieth century allowed Edwin Hubble to open a vast new territory of astronomy. He proved that so-called spiral nebulae were in fact "island universes" or galaxies, far beyond the edges of our own Milky Way. And, as a good scientist, the first thing he did was to start classifying them. His system, published in 1925, categorized galaxies according to their shape—or, in his words, according to how much "conspicuous evidence of rotational symmetry about dominating, central nuclei" they showed. Hubble believed that the shapes revealed the life-cycle of galaxies, and represented this evolutionary system in a chart that later became known as the "tuning fork" diagram for its forked shape.

He believed that elliptical galaxies (class "E"), on the left of the diagram, were the youngest. According to his idea, diffuse and roughly spherical—globular—galaxies flatten into a lenticular or lens shape, from which they grow arms and become spiral (class "S").

The central bulge of some galaxies forms a fat finger of stars and dust—known as a "bar." "Barred spiral" galaxies were given their own class of "SB." Each elliptical galaxy was given a number to describe how round or flattened it appeared. Perfectly round galaxies would be classed "E0," while very flat ones would be "E7." Hubble also used the letters "a," "b," and "c" to note how tightly wound the arms of spiral galaxies were, with "a" the tightest and "c" the loosest.

In the early 1930s, Hubble published classifications of more than 44,000 galaxies. Over the years, as more powerful telescopes were built and photographic methods advanced, the visible universe expanded farther and the astronomical catalogs swelled. Hubble's useful but rough galaxy classification gave way to more sophisticated and detailed work. His idea of evolution—that galaxies change from elliptical types to lenticular types and then to spiral types—no longer fit the new data, and astronomers were forced to give it up. But scientists have kept Hubble's organizational scheme, for even without the evolutionary theory, his system is still the best way to organize the skies.

HUBBLE REVISITED

In 1958, US astronomer William Morgan overhauled Hubble's system. He had already reorganized the field of stellar classification by coding stars by their brightness as well as their color. He rethought Hubble's system and considered how the appearance of galaxies was changed by our viewpoint on Earth. In his system, for example, he included a scale of the angle of the galaxy's tilt relative to the Earth, running from side view (1) to top view (7).

Morgan also delved inside galaxies, linking populations of stars within the galaxy to the types of light they emit. His system of galaxy classification—a, af, f, fg, g, gk, or k—refers to the Harvard star classification order "O B A F G K M." Each letter stands for a different color of star, from hot blue through the rainbow to a cooler deep red. Morgan reasoned that different types of light come from different populations of stars. Older stars in the galactic nucleus—the "Population II" stars—emit reddish light. "Population I" stars, such as the Sun, are hotter, have more heavy elements, and are spread throughout the galactic disk. Hubble classified the Andromeda galaxy, M 31, as "Sb;" Morgan called it a "kS5."

Later astronomers added new dimensions. Two years after Morgan published his new system, Canadian astronomer Sidney van den Bergh assigned a luminosity rating of I–V to individual galaxies. And at about the same time, French-born US astronomer Gérard de Vaucouleurs expanded Hubble's system to take into account the three-dimensional nature of galaxies. But despite all the changes and technological advances, astronomers still swear by Hubble's original system.

HARD EVIDENCE

AN EYE OUT
Modern galaxy classification is fully automated and uses computerized image analysis. A complex program takes into account a galaxy's position, magnitude, color, shape, and other characteristics. One authoritative galaxy catalog, the Sloan Digital Sky Survey, uses an 8.2-foot (2.5 m) telescope and an electronic camera high in New Mexico's Sacramento Mountains (right) to record galaxies. Each of 30 charge-coupled devices (CCDs) in the Sloan camera has four million pixels (picture elements)—twice the number of dots on a high-end computer monitor.

GALACTIC TUNING FORK

Hubble believed that galaxies evolved along a "tuning fork" route, shown here from left to right. His theories were wrong—but his classification system is still used today.

SPIRALS (S)
Spiral galaxies—such as M 33, an Andromeda galaxy satellite of type Sc (left)—are known for the long arms that extend from their central bulge. Hubble classified spirals by how tightly the arms wind around the bulge, from a tight-bound "a" to a loose "c."

Type Sc

Type Sb

Type SBc

Type Sa

Type SBb

Type S0 (lenticular)

Type SBa

Type E5

Type E0

ELLIPTICALS (E)
Elliptical galaxies such as M 49 (right) grade from spherical (0) to oblong (7): M 49 is an E2. They are full of stars, have little gas, and shine uniformly brightly. Hubble thought they evolved into "lenticular" galaxies.

BARRED SPIRALS (SB)
Galaxies such as NGC 1365, (above; type SBb) have a central bar of densely packed stars. These central stars can produce as much as a third of the light from a barred spiral galaxy.

ANDROMEDA GALAXY

By intergalactic space standards, the great galaxy in the constellation of Andromeda is close to the Milky Way—it is 290,000,000 light-years away. Andromeda's majestic spiral is our own galaxy's nearest full-size galactic neighbor. It closely resembles the Milky Way in form and structure, and the distribution of chemical elements in each is so similar that astronomers refer to them together as sister galaxies. But there the similarity ends, for the Andromeda galaxy dwarfs the Milky Way in size and contains around twice as many stars.

ANDROMEDA STATISTICS

DIAMETER	150,000 LIGHT-YEARS
NUMBER OF STARS	400 BILLION
MASS	320 BILLION TIMES THE MASS OF THE SUN
DIAMETER OF NUCLEUS	25,000 LIGHT-YEARS
DISTANCE	2.9 MILLION LIGHT-YEARS
ANGLE OF TILT	13°
OTHER DESIGNATIONS	M 31, NGC 224

ANDROMEDA IN FOCUS

Set among the stars of the constellation of Andromeda, the tiny, misty blur that astronomers know by the catalog number M 31 is easy to miss. Yet despite its unassuming appearance, M 31 is immensely greater than the stars that surround it. For it is an entire spiral galaxy, larger than our own.

For centuries, astronomers thought that the Andromeda galaxy was nothing more than a nebula, a cloud of light-reflective dust and gas situated within the Milky Way. Then, in the 1880s, the English astronomer Isaac Roberts used a 20-inch (50 cm) telescope to take the first detailed photograph of Andromeda. For the first time, the spiral arms were revealed; but since no one could make out any individual stars, M 31 was still assumed to be a nebula. A star suddenly appeared near the center in 1885, but it barely reached naked-eye visibility. Astronomers rightly decided the new arrival was a nova—an exploding star. But they still believed the nebula hypothesis.

Ideas changed after a 100-inch (2.5 m) telescope, then the world's biggest, opened on Mount Wilson near Los Angeles in 1917. The great astronomer Edwin Hubble was able to see for the first time that the outer spiral arms of the Andromeda galaxy contained individual stars. These appeared similar to many found in the Milky Way, but were much fainter. Hubble drew the logical conclusion: M 31 must be another galaxy, lying a great distance away.

Andromeda is especially important for astronomers because it is so similar to the Milky Way. Since both are spirals, with many other features in common, the pair are now described as sister galaxies. Although we can never see our own galaxy from the outside, we can observe our nearby sister instead—the next best thing. At 2.9 million light-years from Earth, Andromeda is the farthest object that can be seen with the naked eye, the distance so great that the visible light began its journey—at 186,000 miles (300,000 km) per second—long before homo sapiens evolved.

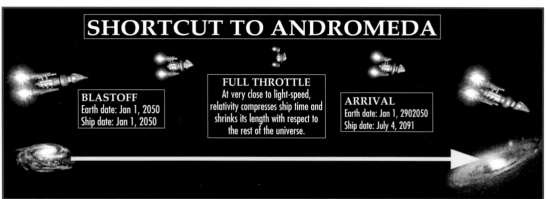

SHORTCUT TO ANDROMEDA

BLASTOFF
Earth date: Jan 1, 2050
Ship date: Jan 1, 2050

FULL THROTTLE
At very close to light-speed, relativity compresses ship time and shrinks its length with respect to the rest of the universe.

ARRIVAL
Earth date: Jan 1, 2902050
Ship date: July 4, 2091

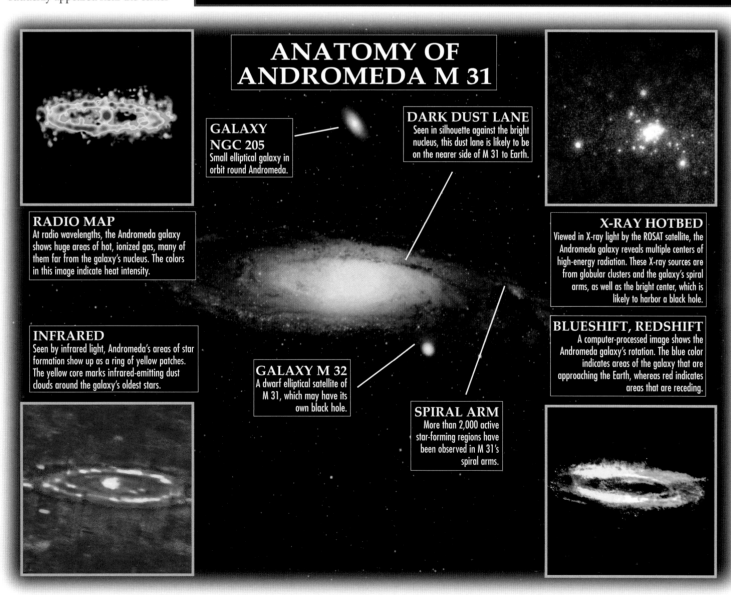

ANATOMY OF ANDROMEDA M 31

GALAXY NGC 205
Small elliptical galaxy in orbit round Andromeda.

DARK DUST LANE
Seen in silhouette against the bright nucleus, this dust lane is likely to be on the nearer side of M 31 to Earth.

RADIO MAP
At radio wavelengths, the Andromeda galaxy shows huge areas of hot, ionized gas, many of them far from the galaxy's nucleus. The colors in this image indicate heat intensity.

X-RAY HOTBED
Viewed in X-ray light by the ROSAT satellite, the Andromeda galaxy reveals multiple centers of high-energy radiation. These X-ray sources are from globular clusters and the galaxy's spiral arms, as well as the bright center, which is likely to harbor a black hole.

INFRARED
Seen by infrared light, Andromeda's areas of star formation show up as a ring of yellow patches. The yellow core marks infrared-emitting dust clouds around the galaxy's oldest stars.

BLUESHIFT, REDSHIFT
A computer-processed image shows the Andromeda galaxy's rotation. The blue color indicates areas of the galaxy that are approaching the Earth, whereas red indicates areas that are receding.

GALAXY M 32
A dwarf elliptical satellite of M 31, which may have its own black hole.

SPIRAL ARM
More than 2,000 active star-forming regions have been observed in M 31's spiral arms.

GLOSSARY

absolute magnitude A measure of the intrinsic luminosity of a celestial body, such as a star, that is expressed as the apparent magnitude the body would have if viewed from a distance of ten parsecs, or 32.6 light-years.

albedo The fraction of light that is reflected off something, such as the Moon or a planet.

aperture An opening that controls how much light passes through a lens, such as in a camera or telescope.

asterism A small group of stars.

binary A system of two stars that revolve around each other under their mutual gravitation.

blueshift The displacement of the spectrum of an approaching celestial body toward shorter wavelengths.

celestial equator The great circle on the celestial sphere midway between the celestial poles.

charge coupled device (CCD) A semiconductor chip with a grid of light-sensitive elements, used to convert light images into electrical signals.

comet An object traveling in outer space that develops a long, bright tail when it passes near the Sun.

constellation A named group of stars that form a particular shape in the sky.

declination The angular distance north or south from the celestial equator measured along a great circle passing through the celestial poles.

double star Two stars that appear close to one another along the same line of sight but that are actually physically separate.

elliptical galaxy A galaxy shaped like an elliptical that contains relatively little gas and dust and has an older stellar population compared to a spiral galaxy.

epoch An event or a time period marked by an event that begins a new period or development.

equinox Either of the two times each year when the Sun crosses the equator and day and night are approximately the same length.

Galactic Center The nucleus of the Milky Way galaxy.

gamma ray A ray that is like an X-ray but has higher energy and that is given off particularly by a radioactive substance.

globular cluster A roughly spherical, tightly packed group of thousands to hundreds of thousands of stars that are gravitationally bound to one another and orbit a galaxy.

halo A bright circle seen around the Sun or the Moon.

infrared Producing or using rays of light that cannot be seen and that are longer than rays that produce red light.

ionization The process of fully or partially converting into ions.

irregular galaxy A galaxy that does not have a distinct regular shape, unlike a spiral or an elliptical galaxy.

lenticular galaxy A galaxy that is classified between an elliptical galaxy and a spiral galaxy in galaxy classification schemes.

light-year A unit of distance measuring the distance light travels in one year.

luminosity The relative brightness of something.

multiple star Several stars located close to one another that appear to form a single system.

nebula A group of stars that are very far away and appear as a bright cloud at night.

nebulosity The relative haziness of something.

neutron star A dense celestial object that consists primarily of closely packed neutrons and that results from the collapse of a much larger stellar body.

nuclear fusion A nuclear reaction in which nuclei combine to form much larger nuclei during which they release energy.

orbit To travel around something, such as a planet or the Moon, in a curved path.

parallax The angular difference in direction of a celestial body, such as the Moon or planet, as measured from two points on the Earth's orbit.

parsec A unit of measurement that is equal to 3.26 light-years and is the distance to an object having a parallax of one second as seen from points separated by one astronomical unit.

photometer An instrument used to measure luminous intensity, luminous flux, illumination, or brightness.

photon The elementary particle of light and other electromagnetic radiation.

plasma A group of charged particles that show some characteristics of a gas but that differ from a gas as a good conductor of electricity and that are affected by a magnetic field.

protogalaxy A cloud of gas believed to be the beginning stage of a galaxy.

protostar A cloud of gas and dust in space that is believed to develop into a star.

pulsar A kind of star that gives off a rapidly repeating series of radio waves.

quasar A very bright object in space that is similar to a star and that is very far away from the Earth and gives off powerful radio waves.

radiation A kind of dangerous and powerful energy that is produced by radioactive substances and nuclear reactions.

recombination The process of electrons and protons forming and bonding together into hydrogen atoms.

redshift The displacement of a spectrum, particularly of a celestial body toward longer wavelengths.

right ascension The arc of the celestial equator measured eastward from the vernal equinox to the foot of the great circle passing through the celestial poles and a given point on the celestial sphere, expressed in degrees or hours; also known as the point of Aries.

sidereal time Time that is measured by the daily motion of stars. A sidereal day is about 4 minutes shorter than a solar day, with hours, minutes, and seconds all proportionally shorter.

solstice One of the two times during the year when the Sun is farthest north or south of the equator.

spectrograph An instrument for dispersing radiation, such as sound waves, into a spectrum and recording or mapping the spectrum.

spiral galaxy A galaxy consisting of a rotating flattened disk with a central bulge made up of mostly old stars, from which two or more spiral arms that are made up mostly of younger stars, interstellar gas, and dust extend.

star atlas A chart or map showing the relative positions of the stars, as seen from the Earth, in a specific part of the sky.

supernova The explosion of a star that causes the star to become extremely bright.

ultraviolet Describing a ray located beyond the visible spectrum at its violet end that has a wavelength shorter than those of visible light but longer than those of X-rays.

X-ray An electromagnetic radiation of an extremely short wavelength that is able to penetrate various thicknesses of solids and to act on photographic film as light does.

FURTHER INFORMATION

BOOKS

Geach, James. *Galaxy: Mapping the Cosmos*. London: Reaktion Books, 2015.

Kanas, Nick. *Star Maps: History, Artistry, and Cartography*. New York: Springer Praxis Books, 2012.

Lang, Kenneth R. *The Life and Death of Stars*. Cambridge, UK: Cambridge University Press, 2013.

Trefil, James, and Buzz Aldrin. *Space Atlas: Mapping the Universe and Beyond*. Washington, DC: National Geographic, 2012.

Waller, William H. *The Milky Way: An Insider's Guide*. Princeton, NJ: Princeton University Press, 2013.

WEBSITES

The Birth of Stars
www.youtube.com/watch?v=9EnBBIx6XkM
In this Youtube video, listen to a short presentation narrated by Steven Hawking on how stars are born.

NASA Astrophysics: Galaxies
http://science.nasa.gov/astrophysics/focus-areas/what-are-galaxies/
This website includes information on the many types of galaxies andD how they form, and also includes recent NASA discoveries related to stars and galaxies.

Space.com: Milky Way Galaxy: Facts About Our Galactic Home
www.space.com/19915-milky-way-galaxy.html
Read all about our home galaxy. This article includes links to stunning photography of the Milky Way.

Starry Night Education: Sky Chart
www.starrynighteducation.com/skychart/
Enter your ZIP code to track the stars and galaxies near your location.

University of Illinois: STARS
http://stars.astro.illinois.edu/sow/spectra.html#sequence
This educational website provides a comprehensive overview of the different kinds of stars, what they are made of, and detailed information on several specific stars in the night sky.

INDEX